THE
AUTOBIOGRAPHER'S
HANDBOOK

THE AUTOBIOGRAPHER'S HANDBOOK

THE 826 NATIONAL GUIDE *to* WRITING YOUR MEMOIR

EDITED *by*

Jennifer Traig

INTRODUCTION *by*

Dave Eggers

A HOLT PAPERBACK
HENRY HOLT AND COMPANY
NEW YORK

Holt Paperbacks
Henry Holt and Company, LLC
Publishers since 1866
175 Fifth Avenue
New York, New York 10010
www.henryholt.com

A Holt Paperback® and ® are registered trademarks of
Henry Holt and Company, LLC.

Distributed in Canada by H. B. Fenn and Company Ltd.

Library of Congress Cataloging-in-Publication Data

The autobiographer's handbook : the 826 National Guide to writing your memoir /
edited by Jennifer Traig ; introduction by Dave Eggers.—1st Holt paperbacks ed.
p. cm.
ISBN-13: 978-0-8050-8713-0 (pbk.)
ISBN-10: 0-8050-8713-3 (pbk.)
1. Autobiography. 2. Biography as a literary form—Study and teaching.
I. Traig, Jennifer.
CT25.A85 2008
808'.06692—dc22 2007047355

Henry Holt books are available for special promotions and premiums.
For details contact: Director, Special Markets.

First Edition 2008

Designed by Elissa Bassist

Printed in the United States of America

1 3 5 7 9 10 8 6 4 2

CONTENTS

APPENDIX

THE
AUTOBIOGRAPHER'S
HANDBOOK

INTRODUCTION

by Dave Eggers

The reasons for writing a memoir are many, but in this introduction I want to talk about one reason in particular, because it trumps all others, I think, and it will, I hope, give fuel to would-be memoirists of any stripe: You should write your story because you will someday die, and without your story on paper, most of it will be forgotten.

Most of what we do as humans—the construction of museums and hospitals and roads and water filtration plants—we do because we want the best possible world for the young people who will inherit it. Paramount among all these gifts we give them is the gift of knowledge—the world's accumulated facts, truths, and wisdom, from the birth of reason and language until today. And yet we're strangely casual about informing our kids about their own families. That is, what children are told about their relatives—their parents, grandparents, and ancestors many and far-flung—is desultory at best. We Americans are particularly forgetful (willfully so, many would say) about our roots. And this is a problem.

As a teenager, I read a book called *Some Recollections of a Busy Life*. It was written by a man named Thomas S. Hawkins, and it was a very funny and altogether fascinating account of a pioneer's journey through mid-nineteenth century America. The author had grown up in Missouri in a very unsupervised, Tom Sawyer sort of way, and then as a young man of twenty-two had set out for open spaces and fortune in California. He led a caravan of covered wagons across the plains, traded with Indians and fought bandits, and finally settled in Northern California, where he helped found the town of Hollister.

This man was my great-great-great-great-grandfather, who my family knew as Great-Granddaddy Hawkins. From a young age I had heard my parents talk about him, primarily because we kept his rifle—that which he had fired at varmints and thieves circa 1860—over the mantel in the family room. Everyone who visited the house wanted to know whose it was and did it still work. It did not.

Beyond the origin of the rifle, all we knew about Thomas Hawkins were scattered bits of his story—until one day, when one of our California relatives sent us a copy of *Some Recollections of a Busy Life*. It had been self-published in an edition of just three hundred copies, but it looked like a real book, with a red cloth cover and durable binding and well-set type. I read it in a few days and was astounded. Here was a man without any formal training in writing—he left school at seventeen—a man who made his living first as a teacher, then as a shopkeeper, and later as a banker, but who nevertheless had managed to write a book that would not be out of place on a bookshelf next to the work of Twain. (He had even grown up a few miles from Hannibal, the home of the former Samuel Clemens.) And because Thomas Hawkins had taken the time to write his story, I had a far deeper understanding of him, his time, my own family history, the life of the pioneers who helped settle Northern California... countless things. He gave us adventure, and romance, and the sound of a wagon crossing Nebraska, and the faces of Indians whom he befriended and of those with whom he fought. In the permanent form of a book, we can learn an astonishing amount about the life Hawkins and others like him led, and we can feel connected to our heritage. (*Heritage*, of course, is not a word commonly uttered in the United States, and it was seldom uttered in our house, but these sorts of things can change.)

The book prompted my older brother Bill to begin a family tree, tracing that side of our family back to England and Ireland and Germany, the tree soon encompassing hundreds of names and dates and hometowns, marriages and children. But beyond these skeletal details, there was no other record of their lives. No books, no journals, no memoirs. And so these people, their lives and voices and knowledge, were lost to us. A sampling of their memories, a sketch of their lives, was presumably passed to their children, and then a faded version of that sketch was passed to the next generation. From there people are reduced to names, dates, perhaps one distinguishing characteristic. The vast majority of what they felt and wanted and saw is gone.

* * *

A few years ago, 826 Valencia undertook a project with an exceptionally innovative teacher named Lisa Morehouse. She taught at Balboa High School, a large public school in the city, and that year she phoned us to see if we might want to send in tutors to help her students with a semester-long oral history project. We jumped in.

The parents of Balboa's students are from everywhere: El Salvador, China, Mexico, Vietnam, Guatemala, American Samoa, Cambodia. In most cases, they are not native English-speakers; add to that the usual lack of communication between teenagers and their parents, and you have a group of students who don't know much about the lives of their forebears. In some cases their mothers and fathers purposely kept their history shrouded, assuming that their children would want to forget the past and start anew.

Enter Lisa Morehouse and her oral history project. Her students were asked to interview a relative who had immigrated to the United States from another country (or, if there were no such relatives, someone who had come to California from another part of the country). The students chose their subject and did a series of interviews, translating them when necessary, and then edited these into compelling narratives.

Along with a dozen or so tutors from 826 Valencia, I went to Balboa one day to help the students edit their narratives. And with the first student I met, I witnessed a revelation. I worked with Jimmy Meas, a Cambodian-American student born in San Francisco, whose father fled Cambodia in the 1970s. Jimmy's father had been a farmer, then a conscript in the Cambodian army, then a servant to the Khmer Rouge. Under that wretched regime, he tried as best he could not to be noticed, not to be sent to the killing fields—until one day he decided to risk all to escape with his wife, Jimmy's mother.

An excerpt from his story:

> I escaped at night with your mother—I met your mother when I was
> about nineteen years old and she was farming rice in the fields—and
> we ran to the forest. That's all I can say. It was dark and cold, windy,
> raining ... You couldn't see anything because there were no lights,
> and our blankets were the clothes we had on. It was scary because I
> didn't know if soldiers were patrolling these areas, and I was scared
> we were going to get caught. I was also scared of bombs, because
> the Khmer Rouge put land mines all over the country...

Jimmy and I read this passage together, both of us astonished. *Did you know all this?* I asked. He shook his head; he hadn't known any of it. His parents had never volunteered the details of their suffering and flight, and he had never before had the platform or inclination to ask them about it. The project made it possible for Jimmy to ask his father to tell his whole story, and as a result, Jimmy's respect for and gratitude toward his parents soared, and his interest in the history of Cambodia was sparked. When Jimmy edited his father's story and 826 published it in the resulting book, *I Might Get Somewhere: Oral Histories of Immigration and Migration*, the process was complete: by recording his father's story, transcribing it and shaping it artfully, he ensured that it would be read, remembered, never forgotten.

* * *

For years now at 826 Valencia, we've been leading workshops for adults who aspire to write their memoirs. I've moderated about a dozen of these panels over the years, and because our attendees requested it, we've given them a good deal of nuts-and-bolts information about not just writing one's autobiography, but publishing it. We've had editors and agents on hand, and their advice was specific and encouraging. But every time we finished a panel, looking out at the fifty or so hopeful and determined faces in the audiences, I knew two things and faithfully conveyed at least the latter: 1) It was unlikely that most of the attendees would find their book published by a mainstream (or solvent) publishing house; and yet 2) Every single member of the audience should write their story anyway. Do it for yourself, I would say—because it's surely as self-revelatory as a decade or so of therapy—and do it for every descendant you've begotten or will beget.

I had been saying this for years, and every time I said it, I would refer to the recollections put on paper by my Great-Granddaddy Hawkins. But I hadn't, actually, read the book since I was twenty-two or so. Now here's a strange thing: When I began to write this introduction, I looked around for a copy of the book, couldn't find it, and ended up buying it from a bookseller in Kansas. And I was floored when I read the first paragraph of the book:

> In writing these recollections, I do so, not expecting or believing that there has been anything in my life that would be of interest to the general public. I trust, however, that my children and grand-children, and their descendants, and a very few dear friends, may desire to know something of the great changes that have taken place in the manner of living in the last seventy years, as well as something of the hardships and privations through which their forefathers passed in that part of our country which was then known as the "Far West."

How nuts is that? I didn't and couldn't have remembered this opening to Hawkins's book, and yet many years later, I'd come to the same conclusion: that you just plain have to put your story down. When memoirs became far more popular—to read and to write—in the 1990s, there was much head-scratching, complaining, and scattershot theorizing about the trend. As is the case whenever a trend arrives—or is perceived to have arrived—little of this hand-wringing was warranted, and most of the theorists posited that the memoir boom would come and go with great alacrity and even shame. But because the memoir trend has hardly abated, and because there are far more would-be memoirists now than probably at any time in human history, it's evidence that there is something deeper happening here.

It has to do with one's right, and even duty, *to write one's self into existence*. Those words, *I write myself into existence*, have been used many times by many writers, and it's debatable who coined the phrase. But I first read the expression when reading Donnell Alexander's *Ghetto Celebrity*, a bold and lyrical memoir from 2003. Alexander grew up in Sandusky, Ohio, the son of an overworked single mother and a wayward hustler of a father. He eventually made his way to Sacramento State University and landed a gig writing for the local weekly, which led to a freelance career and eventually a book contract. Alexander uses the memoir to define his father and himself, to celebrate his family's triumphs and laugh at his and their foibles, all the while setting his own life to the music of language. This is exactly what Whitman had in mind—right?—with "Song of Myself."

Before the memoir boom, there existed the fallacy that the only people who could or should write memoirs were former military commanders, movie stars, presidents—those who had lived on a grand scale, at least historically speaking. This line of thinking forgets, of course, that most of the memoirs we remember and hold dear were written by everyday people, otherwise powerless, who are known to us only because they recorded their stories. What would we know of the soul of a modern-day child soldier if Ishmael Beah had not poured his life into *A Long Way Gone?* Nothing is as effective in bearing witness, nothing is as immediate, as memoir. When, through the rare alchemy of experience and artfulness, the personal becomes universal, there is nothing more power-ful. And one never knows whose story will, through will or chance, give voice to a people or an age.

When a manuscript detailing life during the Holocaust was first dis-covered and submitted to publishers, its interest to the general public was doubted. "Very dull," a reader at Knopf sniffed. "A dreary record of typical family bickering, petty annoyances and adolescent emotions ... Even if the work had come to light five years ago, when the subject was timely, I don't see that there would have been a chance for it." This book was *Anne Frank: The Diary of a Young Girl*. No one, not this editor, not Anne Frank herself, thought that it would become the best-known nar-rative of the six million souls lost in the Holocaust.

The work of Beah and Frank, like that of so many memoirists, was driven by the need to bear witness. The need to say *This happened* and *I lived through this* and *This is what it felt like, this is how I survived*. To write one's story is to offer proof. Even if you haven't seen the horrors some memoirists have, there is nothing like a voice from a page. When someone puts words on paper, and those words are read days or years later, there is an intimacy that cannot be rivaled in any other medium. For those of you who have lost your parents, what would you give to have their life in written form? What would you give for the same from your grandparents? To know them over the course of ten-thousand or one-hundred-thousand words, all of them intimate, confessional, vul-nerable, triumphant? If you have time and want your descendants to know how and why you lived, what drove you and what hurt you, what you saw and what you feared, you need to write it down. In any form it will be invaluable.

* * *

Now, if you can write it down, why not write it well? Putting that extra bit of effort into it, carving here and chipping there, planning a bit before and editing a bit after, might very well ensure that your story is not only read dutifully by a few (or many) relatives, but is enjoyed heartily by anyone who might find it. This is where this guide comes in. The book's editor, Jennifer Traig, has been a tutor at 826 Valencia since its inception in 2002, and has worked on just about every student publication we've undertaken. She's an incredibly generous person, and also a very good memoirist. She managed in her book *Devil in the Details* to make Judaical OCD seem both normal and funny, and in this book she manages, with the help of perhaps the greatest-ever assemblage of modern memoirists—to make autobiography-writing, one of the most seemingly daunting undertakings imaginable, appear approachable to any and all.

My last argument in favor of you writing your story concerns not your children or your responsibility to history, but your duty to yourself. The panelists in this book cover the subject at length, but I'll echo them in saying that as painful as it can be to revisit certain episodes from your past, the process of remembering these periods, and making sense of them and their meaning, and then shaping and reconstructing them—it can be not just therapeutic, it can be absolutely epiphanic. To delve, for a year or years, into your past, with an eye for detail and organization—to look for patterns and signals in your own life and to control its narrative ... What could be more healing than that?

All of the memoirists I have met are startlingly serene people. Begin with Tobias Wolff. Any reader of *This Boy's Life* and *The Barracks Thief* would know that he did not always have the easiest of lives. But when you meet him, and you bathe in his warmth and wisdom and equilibrium, you would quickly and willingly grant him full custody of your kids and pets and home. Even those memoirists who have been through shattering trauma are exceedingly kind, centered, and at peace. Think about Frank McCourt, Anne Lamott, Maxine Hong Kingston; have you met these people? Are there any more self-effacing and reflective people, anyone more serene and willing to listen? I may be overstepping here in attributing all this to their memoir-writing, but I would be surprised if some of their serenity isn't because they spent the time they did sorting out their story, giving shape to their personal narrative, making sense of it all.

So write it for yourself, or yourself plus whoever might find it. Write it as proof you lived, you saw, you suffered, you passed through fire and laughed mightily. Write your life because you lived.

As my final bit of evidence, I offer a final excerpt from Thomas Hawkins's book, which not only shows a man with a wonderfully expansive outlook, but a man who, as a final act of writing of himself into existence, personally published a limited edition of his book. This is how the book ends:

> And as I stand now in the twilight of life and retrospect the past, I feel that I surely have been led by a kind Providence all my days in paths I have not known. I have much for which to be thankful.
>
> There is no one in all the world toward whom I have an unkind thought, and I trust I have the good will of all mankind, and I have been blessed with some kind friends, whose faithful affection has made life worth living and very beautiful.
>
> As I look out on the unknown before me I hope to go on during whatever days of life remain, doing the right as God gives me to see the right, unafraid and trusting implicitly in the love of my Heavenly Father and the hopes of an immortal life beyond.
>
> Until the end may I be able to repeat my favorite motto:
>
> > I live for those who love me,
> > For those who know me true;
> > For the Heaven that smiles above me,
> > And awaits my coming, too.
> > For the wrongs that need resistance,
> > For the right that needs assistance,
> > For the glory in the distance,
> > And the good that I can do.
>
> So here ends some recollections of a busy life, being a sketch of the life of Mr. T.S. Hawkins, of which three hundred copies have been privately published for the author by Paul Elder & Company at their Tomoye Press in the city of San Francisco, in the month of August, nineteen hundred and thirteen.

THE BRAIN TRUST

Meet our experts on the art of the memoir

Every month at 826 Valencia, we gather a panel of published authors before an audience of aspiring writers. For three hours we grill the authors on brass tacks. How, exactly, do they do what they do? How does a vague idea become a completed manuscript? How do they get started? How do they finish? How do they do everything in between, and how do they cope once it's done?

It's a great forum with one major flaw: we can only fit fifty or so people in the building for each seminar. We wanted to bring the experience to everyone else, and that's what we've tried to do in The Autobiographer's Handbook. *We've gathered several dozen of our favorite authors for round-table interviews about the details of memoir-writing, from the most personal and esoteric to the most practical. All will be revealed: how to start and where to start; how to find the story in your story, and how to tell it; how to end and where to end; and what to do next.*

STEVE ALMOND

Steve Almond is the author of two books of autobiographical nonfiction: *Candyfreak: A Journey through the Chocolate Underbelly of America*, about his sugar obsession, personal life, and a changing candy industry; and the essay collection *(Not That You Asked): Rants, Exploits and Obsessions*. His other books include the short-story collections *My Life in Heavy Metal* and *The Evil B.B. Chow*, and the novel *Which Brings Me to You*, co-written with Julianna Baggott.

JONATHAN AMES

Jonathan Ames is the author of three essay collections about his personal life, relationships, and neuroses: *What's Not to Love?: The Adventures of a Mildly Perverted Young Writer*, *My Less Than Secret Life*, and *I Love You More Than You Know*. His other books include the novels *I Pass Like Night*, *The Extra Man*, and *Wake Up, Sir!*

TAMIM ANSARY

Tamim Ansary is the author of *West of Kabul, East of New York*, a memoir of his journey from Afghanistan to America to attend high school on scholarship. He directs the San Francisco Writers Workshop.

ISHMAEL BEAH

Ishmael Beah is the author of *A Long Way Gone: Memoirs of a Boy Soldier*, a personal account of fighting in the 1991 Sierra Leone civil war at the age of thirteen and then later struggling to regain his humanity and reenter the world of civilians. He has spoken before the United Nations, the Council on Foreign Relations, the Center for Emerging Threats and Opportunities, and many other NGO panels on children affected by the war. His work has appeared in *Vespertine Press* and *LIT* magazine.

PAUL COLLINS

Paul Collins is the author of two memoirs: *Sixpence House*, about his family's move to Hay-on-Wye, a village of bookshops in rural England; and *Not Even Wrong*, which explores his son's autism. His other books include *Banvard's Folly* and *The Trouble with Tom*.

FIROOZEH DUMAS

Firoozeh Dumas is the author of two humorous memoirs about the Iranian-American experience: *Laughing Without an Accent: Adventures of an Iranian American, at Home and Abroad*, and *Funny in Farsi: A Memoir of Growing Up Iranian*, a finalist for the Thurber Award for American Humor and the PEN/USA Award in Creative Nonfiction.

STEPHEN ELLIOTT

Stephen Elliott is the author of six books of autobiographical fiction and nonfiction, including *Looking Forward to It,* about covering the 2004 presidential election; *My Girlfriend Comes to the City and Beats Me Up,* a collection of autobiographical erotica; and *Happy Baby,* an account of a traumatic childhood spent in foster homes, which was a finalist for the New York Public Library's Young Lions Award.

JANICE ERLBAUM

Janice Erlbaum is the author of *Girlbomb: A Halfway Homeless Memoir,* about her chaotic adolescence in and out of group homes; and the forthcoming memoir, *Have You Found Her,* about her return to a homeless shelter, this time as a volunteer.

NICK FLYNN

Nick Flynn is the author of *Another Bullshit Night in Suck City,* a memoir of his relationship with his homeless father, and two collections of poetry, *Blind Huber* and *Some Ether.*

ELLEN FORNEY

Ellen Forney is the author of two autobiographical cartoon collections: *Monkey Food,* about growing up in the 1970s; and *I Love Led Zeppelin,* which features her popular "How To" comics, as well as other stories from her life and imagination, ranging from "So Cal Travel Journal" to "My Date with Camille Paglia." She teaches comics at Seattle's Cornish College of the Arts.

LAURA FRASER

Laura Fraser is the author of the travel memoir *An Italian Affair,* about a life-changing trip and relationship begun after the end of her marriage. She is also the author of *Losing It,* a nonfiction exposé of the diet industry.

ELIZABETH GILBERT

Elizabeth Gilbert is the author of the autobiographical travelogue *Eat, Pray, Love: One Woman's Search for Everything Across Italy, India and Indonesia*, about her soul-searching journey undertaken in the wake of a divorce. Her other books include the short-story collection *Pilgrims*, the novel *Stern Men*, and the biography *The Last American Man,* about Eustace Conway.

NICK HORNBY

Nick Hornby is the author of the novels *High Fidelity*, *About a Boy*, *How to be Good*, *A Long Way Down*, and the young-adult novel *Slam*. His nonfiction works include *Fever Pitch*, a book on his life as a devoted supporter of Arsenal Football Club; *31 Songs*, a book about his favorite songs; and *The Complete Polysyllabic Spree*, a book about his reading habits. He has also edited the collection of short stories *Speaking with the Angel*. In 1999, he was awarded the E. M. Forster Award by the American Academy of Arts and Letters.

RACHEL HOWARD

Rachel Howard is the author of *The Lost Night*, a memoir about the emotional aftermath of her father's unsolved murder. She also has a collection of linked short stories and is a member of the San Francisco Writers' Grotto.

A.J. JACOBS

A.J. Jacobs is the author of two memoirs: *The Know-It-All*, an account of a year spent reading the entire Encyclopedia Britannica; and *The Year of Living Biblically*, which details his attempts to live according to Biblical law. He is an editor-at-large at *Esquire* magazine.

DAN KENNEDY

Dan Kennedy is the author of two memoirs: *Loser Goes First: My Thirty-Something Years of Dumb Luck and Minor Humiliation*, about his attempts to find his way in his twenties; and the forthcoming *Rock On*, about his record company exploits. He is a frequent contributor at *mcsweeneys.net*.

MAXINE HONG KINGSTON

Maxine Hong Kingston is the author of *The Woman Warrior: Memoirs of a Girlhood Among Ghosts*, about her Northern California childhood in a Chinese-American home. Known for blending memoir, myth, and fiction, her other books include the National Book Award–winner *China Man*, which tells the story of three generations of Chinese-American men; *The Fifth Book of Peace,* a memoir-fiction hybrid about rebuilding her life after a fire and the loss of her father; and the novel *Tripmaster Monkey: His Fake Book*. She is Professor Emeritus at the University of California, Berkeley.

CAROLINE KRAUS

Caroline Kraus is the author of the memoir *Borderlines*, about the loss of her mother and her destructive relationship with a borderline personality.

GUS LEE

Gus Lee is the author of six books, including the autobiographical novel *China Boy,* about growing up in a Chinese immigrant family in 1940s San Francisco, and the memoir *Chasing Hepburn*, about his family's life in Shanghai during the Chinese civil war. His other books include *Courage: The Backbone of Leadership*, *Honor and Duty*, and *Tiger's Tail*.

BETH LISICK

Beth Lisick is the author of the memoir of a happy-go-lucky suburban childhood and urban adulthood, *Everybody into the Pool*; the short story collection *This Too Can Be Yours*; and a book of poetry, *Monkey Girl*.

PHILLIP LOPATE

Phillip Lopate is the author of several collections of essays about his life in New York, including *Bachelorhood: Tales from the Metropolis, Against*

Joie de Vivre, and *Portrait of My Body*. His other books include a memoir of his teaching experiences, *Being With Children*; a nonfiction account of his trek through his hometown, *Waterfront: A Walk Through New York*; two novels: *Confessions of Summer* and *The Rug Merchant*; and two poetry collections: *The Eyes Don't Always Want to Stay Open* and *The Daily Round*. He is the editor of *The Art of the Personal Essay: An Anthology from the Classical Era to the Present*.

DAVID MATTHEWS

David Matthews is the author of *Ace of Spades*, a memoir of growing up half black and half Jewish in the ghettos of 1980s Baltimore.

FRANK McCOURT

Frank McCourt is the author of three memoirs: the Pulitzer Prize–winning *Angela's Ashes*, about his poverty-stricken Irish childhood; *'Tis*, which continues the story of his life in America; and *Teacher Man*, about his teaching career. He has also published a children's book, *Angela and the Baby Jesus*.

JAMES McMANUS

James McManus is the author of several books, including two memoirs: *Positively Fifth Street*, an account of his experiences at the World Series of Poker; and *Physical: An American Checkup*, which details his experiences at the Mayo Clinic.

AZADEH MOAVENI

Azadeh Moaveni is the author of *Lipstick Jihad: A Memoir of Growing Up Iranian in America and American in Iran*, about her return to Iran as an adult and as a journalist. She is the co-author of *Iran Awakening: One Woman's Journey to Reclaim Her Life and Country* with 2003 Nobel Peace Prize–winner Shirin Ebadi. She is also the Tehran correspondent for *Time* magazine.

DAVID RAKOFF

David Rakoff is the author of two books of personal essays: *Fraud*, about his travels, acting career, and other adventures; and *Don't Get Too Comfortable: The Indignities of Coach Class, the Torments of Low Thread Count, the Never-Ending Quest for Artisanal Olive Oil, and Other First World Problems*. He is a regular contributor to *This American Life* and *The New York Times Magazine*, and is a writer-at-large for *GQ*.

AMY KROUSE ROSENTHAL

Amy Krouse Rosenthal is the author of the memoir *Encyclopedia of an Ordinary Life*, which tells stories from her childhood, family, life, and career in encyclopedia form. She also wrote *The Mother's Guide to the Meaning of Life*, as well as several children's books. She is a contributor to National Public Radio and the host of the radio show *Writers' Block Party* on WBEZ Chicago Public Radio.

MATTHUE ROTH

Matthue Roth is the author of the memoir *Yom Kippur a Go-Go*, about his life as an Orthodox Jew in an unorthodox world, and two novels: *Never Mind the Goldbergs* and *Candy in Action*.

ESMERALDA SANTIAGO

Esmeralda Santiago is the author of three best-selling memoirs: *When I Was Puerto Rican*, about her childhood in rural Puerto Rico and her later move to New York; *Almost a Woman*, which continues the story; and *The Turkish Lover*, about a controlling love affair. Her other books include the novel *América's Dream* and two anthologies of Latino literature co-edited with Joie Davidow: *Las Christmas: Favorite Latino Authors Share their Holiday Memories* and *Las Mamis: Favorite Latino Authors Remember their Mothers*.

JULIA SCHEERES

Julia Scheeres is the author of *Jesus Land*, a memoir of her life with her adopted African-American brother David, detailing their strict religious community and their subsequent stay in a Dominican Republic reform school. As a journalist, she has also written for the *Los Angeles Times*, the *Los Angeles Weekly*, *El Financiero*, and the *San Francisco Chronicle*.

TANYA SHAFFER

Tanya Shaffer is the author of the African travel memoir *Somebody's Heart Is Burning*. A writer and performer, her solo shows include *Miss America's Daughters*, *Brigadista*, and *Let My Enemy Live Long!*

ALISON SMITH

Alison Smith is the author of *Name All the Animals*, a memoir about the aftermath of the loss of her brother, which was named one of the top ten books of 2004 by *People* magazine and won the Barnes & Noble Discover Great New Writers Prize. She teaches writing at Goddard College.

ART SPIEGELMAN

Art Spiegelman is the artist and author of the Pulitzer Prize–winning illustrated narrative of his family's life during the Holocaust, *Maus*, *Maus II*, and the illustrated 9/11 diary *In the Shadow of No Towers*. A longtime contributor to *The New Yorker*, his next book, *Portrait of the Artist as a Young %@?*!*, is an illustrated narrative of his own professional development.

ANTHONY SWOFFORD

Anthony Swofford is the author of the Gulf War memoir *Jarhead* and the novel *Exit A*. He has taught at the University of Iowa and Lewis and Clark College and is a Michener-Copernicus Fellowship recipient.

SARAH VOWELL

Sarah Vowell is the author of four books of personal nonfiction: *Radio On*, about a year spent listening to the radio; *Take the Cannoli*, about American pop culture; *The Partly Cloudy Patriot*, a personal take on American history; and *Assassination Vacation*, an account of her pilgrimages to sites honoring assassinated presidents.

SEAN WILSEY

Sean Wilsey is the author of *Oh, the Glory of It All*, a memoir of his parents' tumultuous divorce and his experiences in alternative schools. His writing has appeared in *The New Yorker*, the *Los Angeles Times*, and *McSweeney's Quarterly*, where he is editor-at-large.

TOBIAS WOLFF

Tobias Wolff is the Ward W. and Priscilla B. Woods Professor of English at Stanford University. His books include two memoirs: *This Boy's Life*, about his life with an abusive stepfather in the Pacific Northwest, and *In Pharaoh's Army*, about his service in Vietnam. His other books include three collections of short stories and several novels, including *Old School*.

Chapter I

MEETING YOUR MUSE

Sifting through your life to find what's worth telling

The old chestnut holds that everyone has one good book in them—and that's probably true—but sometimes, instead, people end up writing the bad book that's in them. Maybe it's their college dorm years reimagined as a sci-fi fantasy. Maybe it's an unhinged, 5,000-page screed against The Man. These things happen when talents are mishandled. All writers take some time to find the right story to tell and the right way to tell it. In this chapter, you'll find your way there, learning how to cherry-pick the part of your life that will make the best memoir.

Let's begin by assuring you that you do have a story to tell. If your life has been ordinary in every way, that alone makes you strange. Some truly wonderful memoirs have been written about perfectly normal lives. Normal doesn't mean boring. It's just all in the telling.

Or maybe you really are an oddball, the albino orphan raised by itinerant drag queens. If so, you've won the memoir lottery. Your book will almost write itself, and your job will be editing it down. When every second of your life has been interesting, the challenge is deciding what, exactly, to focus on.

Or maybe the subject of your memoir hasn't even happened yet. Maybe you're dying to challenge yourself in some way—live in an isolated lighthouse, go a full year without showering, or embark on an all-legume diet—and record the experience in writing. These sorts of experiments have produced some great books, too.

If anything, it's likely you have too many options. Let's start by steering you away from these two right off the bat:

I'm the oldest surviving Lusitanian widow/sweetheart of vaudeville/ Hayes administration cabinet member.

Oldest anything makes the reader assume your book will be creaky, even cranky. Also, because your life has been so long, the reader fears your book will be, too. So if you choose to go down this road, be sure to focus on the especially fascinating parts, ideally involving spies, Prohibition, or the discovery of radium:

I'm the world's youngest brain surgeon/astronaut/discoverer of radium.

Everyone resents a prodigy. Maybe you should spend the next few years wasting your potential shooting craps or watching women's volleyball, then write a book about being a fallen child prodigy instead.

That said, there are no hard and fast rules. There are great memoirs about owning pets, or joining self-righteous cults, or eating grubs. Again, it's all in the telling.

ON FINDING THEIR SUBJECT

ELIZABETH GILBERT: There's a long tradition in English literature of authors using essays as a means of writing their way through some sort of privately tormenting issue or question. This is one of the great benefits of being a writer—that your vocation can also be your salvation. The most striking example of this, I think, is probably the great Robert Burns tome, *The Anatomy of Melancholy*, first published in 1621. This was a giant cinder block-sized lifetime's work, in which Burns tried to sort his way through his depression using research, scholarship, art, science, and, of course, his own writing journey.

My memoir (and many people's memoirs, I believe) was born from the same source—a yearning to write my way out of a dark episode in my life and into a place of comfort and self-comprehension. That said, I didn't want to just sit at my desk and write about my depression and confusion. (Fun read!) Instead, I wanted to turn my memoir into a travelogue of the year I spent crossing the world, trying to find my peace.

As a storyteller, I felt I owed it to my readers not just to sort out my own despair, but to deliver an interesting tale, something worth their time to read. Anything less than that wouldn't have been a proper memoir, but only a sprawling entry from my personal diary of sadness, and I didn't think anyone needed such a thing.

SEAN WILSEY: My subject was growing up (and screwing up). Though I suppose that nobody ever grows up, I only wanted to write about the ways that I more or less had. I only included things in the memoir that I had as-fully-as-possible processed, that were firmly in the past, and that I understood. Of course, I don't know that I understand myself now (and that's why I don't write about myself now), but I understand who I was then, and why I did certain things, and so in the book I talk about things I've pretty well moved through.

TANYA SHAFFER: For me, it was never a question. The year I spent in West Africa was by far the most dramatic and transformational part of my life up to that point. From the moment I returned I was compelled to write about it. It moved me so deeply, I had to get it down, both to share it with others and to clarify it for myself.

FIROOZEH DUMAS: I started writing for my kids, so the first stories I wrote were ones that had some kind of moral. The rest just followed.

RACHEL HOWARD: I knew since about age twenty-one that I wanted to write about my father's murder. I didn't fully understand why I wanted to write about it, because I wasn't really driven to find my father's killer. So I knew what it was about, but I didn't know *how* it was about that subject, especially because most books about murder are whodunits. So I just wrote the material that felt emotionally urgent for me.

One thing that was difficult, though, was deciding how much to weave in from another thread in my life—my stepfather Howdy. Early on in writing the book I showed a chapter about Howdy to my writers group, and one woman gave me some very bad advice: If it's not directly about the murder, don't include it. So for several drafts of the book, I tried to stuff everything about Howdy into one chapter up front. It wasn't until I'd turned in the full manuscript to Dutton [the publisher] and my editor and I were revising that I realized that the book wasn't about the murder—it was about how I reacted to the murder, how I made some peace with it. And the fact that just after my dad's death I'd had to live with Howdy, a sociopath and a drug addict who screamed at me—it couldn't be separated from the full story. That's when I broke that one overstuffed chapter about Howdy into several chapters, spaced out over the full arc of the book, so that that story line could breathe.

ISHMAEL BEAH: It was fairly straightforward for me since writing my memoir came out of a frustration to give context and understanding to what happened in my country, Sierra Leone, and generally the use of children in war. This required me to write about what was before the war, the culture, the people, communities, and how the war destroyed everything.

FRANK MCCOURT: I didn't know until I started. I just started with the first book [*Angela's Ashes*], and it ended up being about my earliest days coming to America, and a little bit about teaching. And then I finished the second book [*'Tis*], which continued the story, and then I did the third one [*Teacher Man*], which was about my teaching career. And that's how it happened. There wasn't any great big plan. I'm not Proust.

NICK HORNBY: I should explain, first of all, that my memoir [*Fever Pitch*] is told through a series of football match reports of games I saw, mostly live, rather than on TV. But only half or less of the book is about football. The other half is about where I was at when I saw these games. When I went with my dad, I could talk about him. When I went with a girlfriend, I could talk about girls, etc. [Finding the subject] was pretty easy: I wouldn't have written the memoir without knowing that, because it was everything. I realized that because my relationship with my football team had been pretty much the most stable relationship in my life, I could tell my story through my fandom.

LAURA FRASER: I had a fairly dramatic experience—my husband left me, I went to Italy to recuperate, I met a French professor on an island who brought me back to life. When I came home, I wrote about it. Over the next three years, to my surprise, we continued the love affair, which ended up healing my divorce. So it was a story where a lot came together: love, healing, travel.

DAN KENNEDY: Me, I generally aim for the parts that I thought were the end of it. Not in a big, grandiose way, but just those moments that seemed like you were going to be stranded with yourself forever and that prospect caused you great concern.

PHILLIP LOPATE: I write about the aspects of my life that are most poignant, funny, and seemingly universal.

ESMERALDA SANTIAGO: Writing memoir is not a question of what the book is "about," but about what happened as I remember it. I begin writing the first thing I remember and go from there. While I write, I find it easier to keep to a chronological timeline rather than to jump around the years or to seek connections until I finish a complete first draft. It is in the process of editing that I know what the book is "about."

DAVID MATTHEWS: I knew that childhood, specifically the years between ages three and ten, comprised the years that sort of cemented one's personality. I also thought that childhood was the last time many of us saw the world as an adventure, a world much larger and scarier than our lived experiences, and that sense of wonder (terror?) works well in a personal narrative. The one thing common to every reader is that they had a childhood—only the specifics vary.

MATTHUE ROTH: I really thought I was going to write about the time when I was fourteen years old, when I was first becoming religious. I had a whole story outline in my head ... but when I sat down to write, I kept getting stuck, and I kept calling friends instead and gossiping about last weekend at the 24th Street bars. That's when I realized I really was on fire to tell a story about my life, only it wasn't the life I was writing about.

GUS LEE: When our daughter was seven, I wrote about being a seven-year-old kid in the [San Francisco] Panhandle. While I was dealing with issues of integrity and character, I wrote *Honor and Duty* and, years later, facing the same issues, I wrote *Courage*. The circumstances of the moment invited memories of a particular past, and I'd hit the keys.

JANICE ERLBAUM: At first, I didn't know what time of my life my book should focus on. I actually wrote a first draft of the book as a series of short stories from various times: age seven, age twenty-four, age eleven, age thirty-one, etc. But that version was rejected by the agents and editors I'd sent it to—they wanted a sequential memoir, a real story, with a beginning, middle, and end. They also noted that the most interesting and dramatic time of my life—the time when my life changed the most—was the time when I was a "halfway homeless" teenager, looking for a stable place to live. This phase started from the minute I walked out of my mother's house at age fifteen, and ended when I got my own apartment at age eighteen. So it seemed clear that there was a nice, natural symmetry there—the book had to start when I left my mother's home, and end when I found a home of my own.

STEPHEN ELLIOTT: I start writing. I'm usually a hundred pages in before I know what a book is about. And then I'm usually wrong.

CAROLINE KRAUS: I came to write *Borderlines* because two experiences had long preoccupied me. I wasn't hunting for material drawn from my life. Far from it—I was more interested in fiction and screenplays than in myself. In my case, the material hunted me down. And when I started laying down the bones of these two experiences, connections surfaced that intrigued me, that seemed to be relevant on a universal level. And that's when I thought I might have a book.

STEVE ALMOND: For my work, the path to the truth always leads through shame. So I tend to focus on the moments that were particularly awful or embarrassing, and kind of run toward the shame, rather than trying to front. But that's just my thing. The general rule is basically to stick to the material that feels most urgent, that documents and investigates a particular obsession.

PAUL COLLINS: Weirdly enough, I consider myself a private person. If I find an aspect of my life that may increase someone else's appreciation of the world, be it old books or understanding autism, then I'll dive right in. But if it's just about me for the sake of talking about myself? I really dislike that feeling.

BETH LISICK: I set out to write a collection of funny stories from my life. It wasn't until my agent was trying to sell it that it became a "memoir."

JONATHAN AMES: I begin with a notion and then build up and tear down, kind of like a sandcastle that, at some point, becomes permanent.

HOW YOU CAN FIND YOUR STORY

JANICE ERLBAUM: Look for the times when your life changed the most, and when you changed the most. Those are the times of peak drama in your life. How did you survive those transitions? Your answers will help others who read your memoir to survive similar transitions of their own.

ISHMAEL BEAH: You have to think about why you want to write about your life, why is it important to do so not only for you, but for others—

the readers? Once you answer these questions, you will find the parts of your life that are relevant to include in your memoir.

PAUL COLLINS: It might not be the part you think, though you may have to write it first to find out. The dilemma always comes down to: there are many reasons to write a memoir, but what are the reasons to read it?

LAURA FRASER: What are the stories you tell your friends? What is something you have overcome and then come to understand in a completely new way? What is a unique experience that you've had that you can universalize to other people?

FRANK McCOURT: You look at the great landscape of your life and you know what was significant and what was boring. It's very personal, what you want to choose. Gore Vidal said a memoir is an impression of your life. It's your impression of your life, and it's yours to do with as you like. It's all extremely subjective.

JAMES McMANUS: Write about the thing you burn hottest about—what you never seem to shut up about at family dinners, intimate conversations, barstool discussions. That's usually a good place to start.

TAMIM ANSARY: You focus on the story-like parts. My premise in memoir is that the quality that we look for in fiction and literature is also there in real life. One is attracted to those events and episodes that seem to have that mysterious quality that reveals something. Looking for the part of your life to write about, it's the heat-seeking missile looking for the story.

JULIA SCHEERES: Memoirs must have themes. They can't just be random pages transcribed from a diary. A specific theme (or themes) helps you organize the material and provides a through-line for the book. A good exercise to discover themes particular to your story is to outline your life in terms of pivotal events and watershed moments. Usually you'll find repeating motifs that you can link and expand on.

DAN KENNEDY: It's always the part you don't want to admit, and the part you don't want to look at. It's the stories that friends want you to tell at dinner, that you wish they'd let you forget, but then as soon as you open your mouth and get honest, you're all laughing so hard you can't eat.

PHILLIP LOPATE: Everyone has a story that churns the guts or that they keep going back to obsessively in their minds. My advice is to write that Big Story, however painful or scary it may be. Also, I would advise aspiring memoirists to write about times when they sinned, not just when they were sinned against, so that the reader can welcome the writer into that universal club of those who add to the world's stock of sorrow.

DAVID RAKOFF: "Aspiring memoirist" is a term that I can't help but find a little bit funny. I sound like an asshole saying this, I know, but memoirs used to be the province of the very old, and in special cases, the very (as opposed to only somewhat) traumatized.

As for advice for the aspiring first-person writer, I'm hopelessly out-of-date here, as usual, what with the kids and their rock and roll and their MySpace and the gradual rendering of such concepts as shame, privacy, and discretion to be as quaint as the Geneva Convention is for the Bush Administration. But I'd urge a little caution before any kind of wholesale, ejaculatory disclosure. I understand very well the wisdom in the adage "write what you know," but it emphatically doesn't mean "write everything you know." But just for oneself as a writer I think what one says is not as important as how one says it. So: parts of your life? It almost doesn't matter, if the writing itself steps up.

GUS LEE: Write about the biggest, scariest darn elephant in the living room of your soul.

JONATHAN AMES: Since I'm a memoirist of sorts, who works incrementally, my tip would be to look at the stories that you often recount to friends or strangers—the real dramatic stories of your life. And the drama can come from pain and joy and embarrassment and triumph and defeat—you know, the usual mix.

STEPHEN ELLIOTT: The most important thing is acquiring pages. Keep writing. Then write more.

ESMERALDA SANTIAGO: I don't believe in making the decision of what part of a life would make the best book before you start writing. It does not work that way for me and I think it leads to false starts and frustration. Begin with the first thing that occurs to you, and keep adding to it, trusting your memory to reveal what is important. Sometimes the most trivial moments end up being the crucial ones in a life, so trust that, if you remember it, it is necessary to set it down. No judgments at this point. Finish a first draft before you start editing the content.

You don't know what your book is about until you finish a complete first draft. It is an organic process that evolves as you become more open and able to recognize what the important moments are and which ones are egotism and vanity. Many writers spend much of their writing time making the first pages or chapters "perfect," without realizing that, often, the book is not "about" the first few chapters, but about a journey that is only understood when you reach the end.

My first drafts are very long, and over the years I have discovered that, often, what I think of as the beginning is mere preparation for telling the real story and often those first few chapters end up deleted.

ANTHONY SWOFFORD: I don't know that people should aspire to write memoir any more than they should aspire to write fiction or poetry. They should aspire to *write*. The genre will be decided by the content.

RACHEL HOWARD: I think if you're an aspiring memoirist, you know which aspects of your life you want to write about—no one wants to write about themselves just because they think they're the most interesting person on the planet, right? It's the how to write about it that's the tricky part. Actually, I sort of take that back—there's a big part of me that really does think I'm the most interesting person on the planet, at least to myself, and I suppose this is probably true for many memoirists-by-nature. And so I do think almost any aspect of my life—or anyone's life—could make a memoir, if it had a compelling shape and emotional honesty.

MATTHUE ROTH: Write about what matters to you. Write about the most dire, pressing, messed-up or embarrassing or nerve-wracking emotional thing you can think of. And, if that doesn't work, just start writing anything. Write about today. See what that reminds you of. And, if that leads you somewhere else, go there. Don't be afraid to follow yourself, and especially don't be afraid of wasting paper or time.

AND IF YOU THINK YOUR LIFE IS TOO NORMAL OR BORING, DON'T WORRY

PAUL COLLINS: You're off to a good start. Seriously: readers appreciate humility, and maybe a sense of amiable bafflement and fascination with others. Those are qualities present in people you'd want to spend time with, and that's what a reader is doing with you. Anyone who actually tells you, "My life would make a great book" ... their life will never make a great book.

If someone is enthusiastic enough about something, that fascination—and not the subject itself—is what the reader will pick up on. Any subject can work, depending on the narrator. I've read great memoirs by retail clerks, and terrible ones by presidents.

AMY KROUSE ROSENTHAL: I don't think there are any boring lives. Not a one. There is only boring prose.

PHILLIP LOPATE: If you think your life isn't interesting enough to write about (which I doubt), you might turn your attention to those subjects you do think are interesting enough, whether it be nature, history, group identity, spirituality, crime, and so on. Then maybe you can begin to see your place in those subjects.

ELIZABETH GILBERT: My tip for writers in general—whether they're writing fiction or nonfiction or poetry or advertising copy—is always the same: "Write what you know. But if what you know happens to be really, really boring ... please, for pity's sake, write something else." In other words, if you honestly believe that your life isn't interesting (not likely, by the way), go out there in the world and do something interesting, and then write about experience. One of my favorite memoirs is *Julie and Julia*, by Julie Powell—a young woman who was bored to death in a dead-end job and a suffocating apartment, who decided to pass her year cooking every single recipe in Julia Child's *Mastering the Art of French Cooking*. Then she wrote about that experience. Her dead-end job was still dead-end, her suffocating apartment was no less suffocating, but she had a great story to tell now, and she told it wonderfully.

ANTHONY SWOFFORD: Write about normalcy and boredom. I did.

BETH LISICK: The "normalness" of my childhood became the thing that people focused on because it seemed so unusual. I'd say just write what is true to your experience. It might not be as "normal" as you think it is. Also, I am a firm believer that everybody has a story to tell. When I hear people complaining about the "glut" of memoirs by people who haven't "done anything," it seems elitist. People read for a lot of different reasons and there's probably somebody out there who will connect with your experiences or storytelling style.

JONATHAN AMES: I've seen in my classes that almost any closely observed situation, even the most banal, can be brought magnificently to life by putting down one's feelings, anxieties, and emotions, as well as analyzing and looking closely at the behaviors of the other players in that particular moment. Also, if your own life is boring, the lives of others are almost always fascinating—just get someone talking and the stories that come forth, in the person's particular vernacular, are usually quite amazing.

DAVID RAKOFF: Claudia Shear, in her terrific one-woman show, *Blown Sideways Through Life*, admonishes the audience against dismissing others. "No one is ever just a waiter," she says. If you take the time to listen, everyone has a story that would stop your heart. But not having a story that would stop someone's heart is actually a very, very good thing! Hold on to that carefree existence as long as you can. Life is an equal-opportunity shit-kicker and you'll have them soon enough and they're not always super fun to live through once, let alone again, when you sit down to commit them to paper. Moreover, they are not required for being a writer. Being a writer is a requirement for being a writer. Write about anything. Set yourself assignments. Go out and cover something as if you were on an actual story. Learn how to be a reporter, how to absent yourself from the narrative, how to stand quietly with a notebook and let the stories of others come to you. They won't all be double-murder car accidents. Learning to create a narrative out of something mundane, how to take those notes and curate the details, will invariably teach you something about how to write your own less-than-cataclysmic life.

JANICE ERLBAUM: If you think your life has been too normal or boring to write about, join the club. Most of us feel that way. But writing a memoir is not about entering a contest to see who had the worst or the strangest life; it's about honestly communicating your emotions so that other (normal, boring) people can feel less alone on the planet. Most of us have experienced sadness, exhilaration, betrayal, sickness, or even the death of a loved one; that's all part of a "normal, boring" life. Whatever's happened in your life will be interesting to other people who are facing the same experiences. Memoirs don't have to be about death or tragedy; they can be about life and love.

CAROLINE KRAUS: Reaching even young adulthood requires passage through so many meaningful and universal experiences that being boring or normal probably isn't what's holding you up. The particulars of what happen in a memoir are less important than the meaning the author draws from those events.

ALISON SMITH: In 1996, I took a summer writing workshop at a college in Vermont. My teacher was Rick Moody. Rick took me aside one day and told me that my stories were well done. "But," he said, "I don't care. They're distant and cold. Why don't you write about something you know, something from your own life?"

His advice threw me. I stopped writing for a while after that workshop. I reread my journals instead. (There were a lot of them—I had been keeping a diary since high school.) What I discovered was that when I was writing for myself, when I was not thinking about creating "literature," I wrote about my family, about my brother Roy, about everything we had and everything we lost when he died.

If you look closely enough you will find that no one's life is "normal." Still, I certainly didn't think that anything of note had happened in my life. I still sort of think that nothing of note really happened to me, especially if you're comparing my life to great political movements or the history of nations. But then if you are thinking about great political movements or the history of nations, *please stop*. That sort of thinking rarely leads to good memoir writing.

STEVE ALMOND: Everyone on this planet has a rich internal life, one filled with unbearable desire and torment and guilt and rage and mercy. That's our inheritance. Modern capitalist culture makes a great effort to replace this internal life with a series of frantic buy messages—because this keeps the profits healthy. But even those people working so hard to be superficial are deep. Frightened, self-censoring, in retreat—but deep.

LAURA FRASER: Go do something interesting.

MATTHUE ROTH: One person's *Ulysses* is another person's ... well, *Ulysses*. The person I know who most professes to be boring is the one who breeds worms, gets arrested routinely (this is an eighty-year-old man, by the way) and worked his way across the country a few years ago by walking into bakeries and taking over operations for a day. The act of writing is the act of forcing people to fall in love with what you love. And the way to do that is by showing why you love the things you love.

A.J. JACOBS: I have to say, a normal life can be a problem. If you're a phenomenal writer like Bill Bryson [*The Life and Times of the Thunderbolt Kid*], you can pull it off. His memoir about growing up in the '50s doesn't have any abuse or addiction or Irish poverty, but it's riveting nonetheless. Still, that's the exception to the rule, I think. I am burdened with a relatively normal and boring life. So I decided that I had to put myself in extraordinary situations, which is how I came to read the encyclopedia [*The Know-It-All*] and grow excessive facial hair [*The Year of Living Biblically*]. Plus, writing the memoir of a normal life can quickly devolve into an exercise in navel-gazing and self-absorption. Having a huge topic in addition to myself (knowledge or religion) helps save me from that.

FIROOZEH DUMAS: A good story does not require an extraordinary event. It just requires an eye for detail.

DAN KENNEDY: I know day-to-day life is boring. Mine is a lot of times, anyway. Life gets interesting when you start to look at the highlights over twenty or thirty years, but sure, your average Tuesday will drive you up a wall half the time. On the other hand, I wish everyone could see how they have a story. I wish everyone could see that they have their own legacy, but most folks only give that credit to some celebrity in a magazine. I mean, you got here. As boring as an average Monday or Tuesday might be, you're in the show—biologically, the odds were stacked against you being the good egg, but you were it, my friend. Standing on this planet is to have won a lottery.

NICK HORNBY: Well, nothing had happened to me [before *Fever Pitch*]. But that was kind of the point. I took the view that fandom is both entirely commonplace and, looked at in a different light, absolutely extraordinary. And I felt that I could represent a certain kind of guy. If my life or my fandom had been unusual then the book wouldn't have worked. The more I thought about it, the more I saw that I had participated—in an entirely unconscious and very modest way—in the social history of my country—as have we all.

And any life can be made interesting by jokes. If you've had a normal, boring life, then be funny about it.

ISHMAEL BEAH: I do not believe that anyone has a normal or boring life. Our day-to-day experiences and human interactions are so fascinating, complex and filled with wonders, that if we stop to closely pay attention to them, we can no longer think of our lives as boring or normal.

Chapter II

PRECURSORS TO THE PAST

Pearl diving in the depths of your life

There are good reasons to start by doing research. It lets you kill a little time while you work up the courage to start writing. It gives you something to do while the bigger ideas incubate. And if you're having trouble getting started, research can provide the early bricks from which you'll build your memoir. Remember, you're not inventing the wheel; there are lots of books already written that you can draw on for inspiration. Read some for style, others for background. It all goes into the stew, and it all helps.

Also, unless you have a photographic memory (material for a memoir in itself), there's a pretty good chance you forgot some things. Looking through old yearbooks, listening to the albums you wore out in school, scrolling through microfiche and leafing through back issues of Time *or* Tiger Beat—*activities like these are not just procrastination. They help shake the dust off the memories buried in the way back of your brain. And then there's the great resource that is other people, experts and bystanders, who can help fill in your story with things their brains have hung onto for whatever reason over the years.*

Research also helps you connect to the larger world, an important part of any memoir. The only people who want to read a book that's all about you are you and perhaps your mother. Background materials make the book bigger and the reader more invested. So if your memoir is about psoriasis, some background on the history and science of the disease will make your story more meaningful, complete, better.

Of course, the thought of scrolling through microfiche and interviewing derma-
tologists can be unpleasant as well. But bear in mind that you're not writing a comp-
rehensive history of the world—just a history of how you fit into it all. You only
need a certain amount of background, and there are lots of tools to make gathering
it easier. In this chapter our authors offer their most effective research methods.

ON RESEARCH

SEAN WILSEY: I did a ton of research. I worked at *The New Yorker*, and
saw how rigorous the research was there—all the reporting and fact-
checking that goes into every story. I wanted to apply these techniques
to my own story, and use them to get to as accurate a point of view as
possible. So I did a ton of interviews. Everyone I talked to would give
me a few more details about a given event, and then I would compress
all those details into scenes.

I did a lot of newspaper reading. Going back and looking at old newspapers, reading stories about the San Francisco earthquake or my parents'
divorce, it was amazing how old newsprint could still tell a story.

My own memories are the most important thing, but the more stuff
I could get in from other sources, the more I felt it was a relevant,
fleshed-out narrative.

SARAH VOWELL: This is way obvious, but, in writing about history,
primary documents like diaries and speeches, as well as, say, contemp-
orary newspaper accounts of one's subject's words, are the best and most
useful treasures. That said, don't trust anyone! Try and figure out what
the person *isn't* saying, too. Especially political and religious figures.

LAURA FRASER: People don't understand that you have to research
your own memoir. But since mine was a travel memoir, I did a lot of
research about the history, literature, and little quirks of each place we
visited. It added a whole new texture. I was also careful to make the
Italian meals and language accurate and authentic.

RACHEL HOWARD: For me, research and writing went hand-in-hand, and sometimes the research process—like looking up old newspaper stories about my father's murder, stories I'd never read—became part of the tale of facing his death.

JONATHAN AMES: I'm not much of a researcher. I'm more of an experiencer—I'll do something and then write about it in my journal or remember it; that's the extent of my research. My biggest preparation is to read the writers I love and to try to mimic their styles, depending on the piece, and depending on which writer I'm most entranced by at that time and want to mimic.

NICK FLYNN: Generally I don't do research until after I have exhausted my memories, for the interesting thing about memoir is how your memory transforms the past. Anyone could Google some historical fact to find "the truth," but that's not why we read memoirs. That said, at some point research is essential, if only to layer what you remember, to see where you misremembered.

MATTHUE ROTH: I always try to have as much firsthand material ready as I can—old journals, menus, ticket stubs from concerts, programs of shows I performed in. I also pore through my old calendars like a maniac. When writing a memoir, it's important not to be *too* focused on details—articles can easily get bogged down with too much information; memoirs even more so—but I'm a nut about continuity. I like to make sure the passage of time holds together at least mostly. If I can have Thursday night concerts really happening on a Thursday night in the book, I'm golden.

PHILLIP LOPATE: I now research much more than I did at the beginning of my essay-writing career. I find that almost any subject can be enriched by delving into the subject. In my book *Waterfront* [a book based on two Manhattan walks, one up the west side and one up the east], for instance, my research took me into history, politics, ecology, engineering, architecture, literary studies, law, and so on. If the reigning formula for autobiographical writing is Self Meets World, research can help supply us with the second part of the equation. I go to the library or order books online.

TOBIAS WOLFF: It depends. I did a lot of research before the writing of *Old School*. It deals with three real and distinct writers, and I steeped myself in their work and reminiscences by people who knew them, in their biographies, their letters. I immersed myself as best I could in the atmosphere of those times. That is seldom necessary with a short story because you're generally not creating the picture of an age.

FRANK MCCOURT: Everything you need to know is in your head, unless you want other people's opinions, which I didn't want. I wanted my own vantage point. I had been scribbling in notebooks for years, but when it came time to write I didn't use them. I just went back into my own memory chip.

NICK HORNBY: I didn't do anything. I've seen hundreds of Arsenal [soccer] games, and forgotten a lot of them. But the ones I remembered were because there was something to say about them. Maybe I went with someone weird (for example my stepmother, who I'd only just met), or maybe it was a game where Arsenal won a championship, or there was a particularly memorable riot … so the games I wrote about selected themselves. I checked the scores afterwards, but I didn't really need to. I have a worryingly good and possibly moronic memory for results of games.

CAROLINE KRAUS: I had calendars, photographs, family archives, and family members to help me organize timelines and facts.

TANYA SHAFFER: I kept extremely detailed journals during my time in West Africa and drew heavily on those when writing my memoir.

For details I couldn't remember and didn't record, especially physical details like plants, birds, and landscape, I used the amazing Internet.

ANTHONY SWOFFORD: I reread a number of the war memoirs from earlier twentieth-century wars and published histories of the Gulf War, as well a few compilations of the journalism from the era. I also reread the military manuals I'd been trained with.

DAVID RAKOFF: It depends on what I'm writing. If it's a reporting trip, I certainly try to read up. Also, and this is very important, nothing succeeds like a well-padded frame of reference. You are your own library. Writing is a completely associative act. If something triggers an Elizabeth Bishop poem or a snatch of movie dialogue—something I rely on far too heavily in my own writing, I know—it only makes it richer. It's a mainstay of Japanese literature, actually; using phrases of homonyms that evoke ancient classical Chinese poetry. It doubles and deepens the resonances, *blather blather yawn*, but you get the point.

Writing is a craft. The greater selection of tools at your disposal, the more artful the result. The more stuff you have at your fingertips (and as is happening lately, the more stuff you seem to forget on a daily basis), the better. You are the only person who can do that.

ON USING MEMORY TRIGGERS

FRANK McCOURT: I don't need to because the memories are so vivid. I remember my baby sister dying, and twin brothers dying; I remember my father being drunk, my mother's despair, what it was like to sit in our kitchen eating dry bread and drinking tea. And I remember all the funny things that happened, funny neighbors and characters, priests, schoolmasters, policemen, politicians, getting my first job … it's all very vivid.

STEPHEN ELLIOTT: Sometimes I use photographs; describing a photograph can be a great way to start writing about something.

NICK FLYNN: I use whatever I can. Returning to the scene of the crime seems essential, whether as a road trip or in dreams.

DAN KENNEDY: Music. If you're writing about the past, put on the songs you listened to then and suddenly all the details you didn't know you had inside of you all start coming back.

ISHMAEL BEAH: Before writing I would listen to Sierra Leonean music or some type of African music that would bring me that landscape. I needed the nostalgia as a motivation and memory trigger; music often did that for me.

RACHEL HOWARD: I used music—a lot. I got a Rod Stewart *Greatest Hits* collection, and listening to the old songs brought a flood of memories back to me—I was four years old again, back in that house with my dad. I could see the furniture, feel the summer heat, hear things he'd said to me again.

I then thought about why my father had been such a Rod Stewart fanatic, and started to think Rod's rock-and-roll swagger held some truth about who my father had wanted to be. Then I realized that I'd actually avoided Rod Stewart songs for more than a decade—felt a wave of ickiness and fear if one came on in the grocery store—because I couldn't handle the memories yet. Listening to Rod Stewart—whom I'd long considered silly and washed-up—became a way of reclaiming my dad. And my *aide memoire* ended up feeding a lot of the material in the book.

I also used pictures a lot. I have a favorite shot of me sitting next to my father, and the sun is striking us in just such a way that I can feel it on my skin, feel myself sitting next to him on that hot summer day. I flipped through old albums, dug through boxes of forgotten pictures. A badly composed throwaway shot can contain some tiny detail—the gold necklace my dad was wearing, the business logo on the side of his van—that is so specific that the past feels real and vivid again, and so much else comes back.

DAVID RAKOFF: Movies, certainly. Artworks, undoubtedly. Music not as much. And food, of course. Always food. To a near-pathological degree, food. Food means everything, sadly. I was at supper recently with people I hadn't seen in years. We were trying to work out when the last time had been exactly, and while I couldn't be quite sure when (it had been four years), I was able to say with utter clarity to the hostess, "You made a daube of beef with mashed potatoes." People looked at me with a little bit of a "what kind of no-life loser remembers a meal from four years ago?" look. Well, *this* kind of a no-life loser does.

ANTHONY SWOFFORD: I used pictures, a journal, and my military gear. *Jarhead* opens with me going through a rucksack, unpacking my past.

BETH LISICK: We have got a lot of great family slides that I love to look at.

TANYA SHAFFER: Other than my journals, I looked a lot at photos, both my own and other people's, to take me back to the feeling of the particular place.

PHILLIP LOPATE: When it comes to summoning a memory, the best method for me is just to relax and invite what comes. For instance, in those moments of the morning when I first wake up, my mind is relaxed and I point questions to it. I also find long train rides to be a stimulus to memory.

JANICE ERLBAUM: I kept all my old notebooks, letters, pictures, and calendars from my high school years, and went through boxes and boxes of archives in order to jog my memory about events that had taken place fifteen or twenty years prior to the writing of the book. I also returned to the shelter where I used to live—re-entering the physical space was one of the most helpful things I did to remember that time of my life.

The *smell* of the place brought back so many emotions that had been buried, and I was able to be much more specific about the environment I was writing about. I also listened to the songs that were popular back then, which brought back many memories.

FIROOZEH DUMAS: I strongly believe in memory-triggers. Smells and music really bring back memories. Oddly enough, so does soaking in the bathtub. I can't explain that one.

CAROLINE KRAUS: Music can jump-start me sometimes, and get me in a particular, desired mood. But it can be risky for me to write under the influence, too. Sometimes when the product is read in silence it's clear I was relying on Otis Redding or Nina Simone to do most of the work. When I take walks with my dog I always take a notepad. I daydream when I walk, and that can be very productive.

MATTHUE ROTH: Old photo albums are a great treasure. Not just the photos themselves, but the memories around them—the taking of the pictures, the people in them, the people who aren't in them. I have one photo that's just an orange blur, of a bonfire that somebody made on the south lawn of my high school in twelfth grade. Backgrounds of photos are especially helpful: Who's hooking up with who, who's making severe eye contact with someone else ... and who isn't.

ALISON SMITH: At first what I discovered was how much I had forgotten. But as I looked more closely I realized that I had not so much forgotten as locked away certain memories. Much of writing a memoir is about the act of remembering. When the memories started to come back to me, they were so vivid and visceral that I could not manage them easily. I cried a lot. This is something that is overlooked quite often in the teaching of memoir. It's deeply emotional work and getting a handle on your emotions is part of that work.

Excuse the new-agey tone of this next comment but it must be said: Be gentle with yourself. Most people who are writing memoirs these days are writing stories that someone told them never to tell, they're writing back to themselves. If this is you, remember that on some days the emotions can be overwhelming, they can lead you to believe that you will never be able to do this.

No one is required to keep going if it gets too hard, but if you do decide to keep going, remember that dredging up memories and emotions is harrowing work. I spent a lot of time just slogging through the intense images that were coming to me. Creating a narrative structure out of all these disparate and powerful images was my biggest challenge.

JULIA SCHEERES: I used all kinds of sensory triggers. Because I was writing about rural Indiana in the '80s, I immersed myself back in that world as much as possible. I listened to Duran Duran and the Police, burned clover candles, bought the same shampoo I used in high school, started eating mayonnaise again, bought a bottle of Love's Baby Soft perfume, etc. And I made a special album of photos from that time.

Taking trips back to Indiana, and to the Dominican Republic (where I compiled a whole separate list of memory triggers) were invaluable. I went back to both places and investigated the surroundings like a reporter, jotting down notes on everything from how people talked, to the smell of my old church basement (it stunk of mildew, just as I remembered it), taking video footage, visiting my old haunts. Talk to people you knew at the time and pick their minds for their recollections of people and events. The floodgates will open, I promise.

Here's a tip: write down the five senses (sight, smell, hearing, taste, touch) and next to them, triggers for your life.

ON INTERVIEWS

PHILLIP LOPATE: I often conduct interviews with experts. I recommend it. Hey, they know a lot and can even point me to the best written sources. I can also try out my cockeyed hunches on them and see if I'm in the ballpark.

DAVID RAKOFF: I do a lot of interviewing, but again, it depends on the piece you're writing. Actually, scratch that. Having another voice is almost always a good thing; a nice breath of new air. It can lend authority, or provide a much-needed corroboration, or refutation. If the goal is to try to find the universal in the personal—and I think it is—then having more than just your own viewpoint can only be good.

RACHEL HOWARD: The "interviews" I conducted became the final third of the book—me finally talking to my grandparents and uncles about the murder after so many years of the subject feeling taboo, finally seeing my former stepmother—the woman who was sleeping next to my dad when he was stabbed—after seventeen years. The final third of my memoir is very reflexive—it's me as an adult trying to piece together the story, finally piecing together a narrative that feels whole to me, finally fully remembering my dad. In a sense, it's about the writing of the book. I did not take notes during these interviews. I didn't need the interviews for gathering research so much as I needed to live them. Obviously this strategy was very particular to the emotional needs that were driving my writing.

NICK FLYNN: Along with interviewing my father, at some point I interviewed a sample of people who knew him at various stages of his life. What I found interesting was that everyone had a differing perspective on him, on why he did what he did, on whether he was an artist or a fraud. In the end it seemed more telling about those I interviewed than about my father.

MATTHUE ROTH: There's a line from *Lost Highway*, the David Lynch movie, that goes something like this [paraphrased]: "I like to remember things the way I remember them, which is the opposite of what happened." If you need interviews to jog your memory, go for it; remember, however, that you're diluting your memories—which also includes your primal emotional feelings. Once you write the scene, or you're stuck for plot points ... then you can pull in other people.

If you *do* feel the necessity to do interviews, then you should start writing either: a) as soon as you talk to the person, so it's fresh in your head; or b) a generous amount of time after the interview, to give you distance from it. Try out both techniques; see which works better for you.

ANTHONY SWOFFORD: After completing the book I tracked down a few members of my unit to confirm certain events. For a personal memoir I don't think interviews are necessary. Other voices will simply bog down the writer. If others don't like what you've written, tell them to write their own book. Most likely they won't.

NICK HORNBY: I didn't speak to a soul, and I'm glad I didn't. The first part of the book is about my relationship with my dad, which wasn't so great at the time. I was unhappy, and that's what I wrote about. But when he read the book, it was clear he didn't remember it like that. If I'd interviewed him, I'd have felt obliged to accommodate his version, and it would have wrecked the tone. And for what? I was unhappy, whatever he thought. The book was about what it felt like, and it wasn't my job to include his perspective. He can write his own book. I have found with both fiction and nonfiction that if the facts don't matter (a big if) then research frequently does more harm than good.

JONATHAN AMES: If I'm sent by a magazine to cover something— like the U.S. Open or a Goth music festival, to give two examples—I, naturally, do interviews. For writing memoirs, I think it's very useful to go to the people who were involved and interview them, to make sure your memory of the story/situation is accurate, and to get someone else's take as well.

LAURA FRASER: I didn't interview people for my memoir, but every memoir is different. If, say, you're trying to reconstruct a part of your life, it would be invaluable to talk to the people who were there.

JANICE ERLBAUM: I didn't interview anybody from my past, but I had their input anyway, as I'd saved all their notes and letters. I didn't want to hear what people thought about the events now; I needed to know how they felt about the events at the time when they were happening. If there's something you don't remember, and you don't have any records from that time, then by all means, ask people who were there. But don't expect them to be able to recreate their feelings of ten or twenty years ago—the biases they have today will influence their recollections.

AZADEH MOAVENI: I had lots of informal conversations with my family, and this helped enormously. For me, talking was really key to shaping my themes and discovering what I actually wanted to say.

SEAN WILSEY: You have to ask endless questions. There are a few stories in the book about my uncle Jack, who was kind of a wild man— having once broken up a cocktail party, I learned, by firing a Tommy gun into a fireplace—but I'd never really gotten any specifics. So then I started asking around, talking to people who'd known him and my dad, and the stories, as evidenced by the above, were much weirder than I ever expected them to be. I think every family has some nutty (and dark) stories like that. But until you really start asking questions, you just have no idea.

BETH LISICK: I would call up my family or my childhood best friend and ask questions. What night of the week was Family Night? What year was the first Ladies Luncheon? Stuff like that. Sometimes it was helpful, like when they were able to give me a detail that I had forgotten, but other times it was frustrating if I remembered something one way and they remembered it another.

In the end, unless my brother had overwhelming evidence that there was no Cool Whip on the Jell-O, I would go with how I remembered it. I recommend writing what you're going to write first, the way you remember it, and then asking questions later.

TANYA SHAFFER: I sometimes talked informally with West Africans, or others who had visited West Africa, to get their perspective on the stories I was telling and check my memories of certain episodes and periods against theirs. For the most part, though, I relied on my memory. Whether you should conduct interviews would really depend on the type of book you're writing. Memoirs run the gamut, from highly personal essays to near-fantasy to something approaching journalism. If you think outside perspectives would enrich yours, by all means go for it.

DAN KENNEDY: You know, there's something a little too precious in my opinion, about sitting down with, say, my dad, and going—"Okay, listen, I'm writing a book and you're in it, so let's get some details on the record here." I mean, ultimately writing is a really humbling job, not an excuse to take license with others or put people on the spot. I'm not talking about journalism or scholarly works that require that kind of research and diligence; I'm talking about writing a funny memoir.

In my experience writing will be the most humbling job you've ever had. I'm surprised so many of us want to do it. Can you imagine? If somebody said they've got a great job for you but that the only catch is that the hours are midnight to midnight, seven days a week, the pay varies wildly and is not guaranteed, the responsibilities are many, and you report to almost everyone you know or meet? And then they were like, "Oh, and P.S.: if you can leave the party early or skip it all together, that would be great, because you need to go over your marked-up manuscript again and key in revisions to the copyedit." The weird thing is, it'll be one of the best jobs you've ever had.

ON DEPICTING SETTING

TANYA SHAFFER: I do free-writes in which I try to conjure memories involving all of my senses: sight, sound, smell, touch, taste. Then I cull through those and find the most unique and evocative images. It's about choosing the right one or two sensory details that conjure a place very specifically. A little bit goes a long way.

PHILLIP LOPATE: I have written about New York City all my life: it's probably the main character, next to myself, in all my books. Since New York is so various and complex, I don't try to capture all of it in any one piece, and I shy away from large generalizations. My strategy is additive: a corner here, a fragment there, till they add up to a larger picture.

In general, place is a very promising theme for memoirists and personal essayists to explore. It doesn't have to be a major metropolis; any place becomes the intersection of world and character. One exercise might be to take walks and describe the place. Walking-around literature is a rich tradition. Another might be to research the history of the place. A third is to interview and write profiles about some of the old-timers.

TANYA SHAFFER: My advice is to keep extremely detailed journals. Sit in a roadside cafe for an hour and write down everything that's going on around you. Record conversations verbatim at the end of the day to keep the rhythms and melodies of the area's speech in your head. Write down unusual place names and words with great sounds. If it helps get you going, write your thoughts out to friends in letters, and ask them to save them for you. A lot of the material in my book came out of letters I sent to my boyfriend and to my best friend.

Research can help, too. The more you know about a place's history and culture before you go, the richer the perspective you'll have to draw on when taking things in and interacting with local people. You can then bring all that richness to your account of the experience.

LAURA FRASER: So many people want to write about travel. I think that place has to be the setting for the story, not the story itself. Nothing is more boring than a travel narrative that says we went here and then there and saw this and then that. The place should evoke emotion. How the character sees the place and reacts to it reveals his or her state of mind.

Also, contrasts in places can serve to bring out character: it's one thing to have an affair on an Italian island, and another to be together driving on the L.A. freeway.

I took a lot of notes and photos while I was traveling, and also read a lot about the places, so I felt quite immersed. I try to take notes about my senses when I travel, and jot down specific plant names, foods, places—the more specific, the better.

ELIZABETH GILBERT: Don't be intimidated by the fact that others may have already written about this place before you got there—or even before you were born. One third of my book is about Italy—do you have any idea how many people have written about Italy? Famous people, brilliant people, *Italian* people, scholars, poets, historians, foodies, experts—people much more "qualified" than me had already gone to Rome and tried to describe it.

How can I compete with Byron, with Henry James? I can't. So I didn't. I wrote my own book, from my own experience. This doesn't mean I don't have an obligation to be as accurate and informed a writer as possible (I read Byron and Henry James before I started writing about Rome) but at some point you have to believe that your interpretation of a place is just as valid as anyone else's.

I met a young writer recently who told me that her "dream of dreams" was to travel around the world visiting holy sites from various world religions, and writing about her experience. Sounded great to me. But then the girl sighed and said, "But that's been done already." What I told her was, "Yes, but it hasn't been done yet by *you*."

There isn't a story out there which hasn't already been told in some form or another; humans are storytellers and we've been doing this for a long time. But your version of the story has never been told before, and so it's different and special and elegant and important in its own way.

No subject is ever completed; nobody gets the last word. So don't try to win this by going on some kind of crazy, twisted search for the place on earth that has never been visited, or the travel story that has never been written.

Find instead your dream-of-dreams, go to that place, and tell us what happened to *you*.

Chapter III

YOU vs. PAGE ONE

Having started, starting

There may be no literary form that lends itself to procrastination as much as the memoir. When you're writing about your life, the temptation to just go live it is overwhelming. Somehow, spending half a day watching talk shows becomes research; going for a beer at 3 p.m. is gathering material. It's an awfully nice day, who knows what could happen—what say you take the rest of the afternoon off?

Eventually, however, if you want to be a writer, you'll have to write something. Yes, it's true: there's little as daunting as the blank page. There's the fear that everything you write will suck, and the dread that even if you manage one good page you'll still break under the weight of the 199 blank pages that will have to be filled after that one to make a book. And even if you do finish it, there's the dread of finding an agent and a publisher, and then the dread of bad reviews, and then the dread of a follow-up, and what if the movie adaptation sucks, too?

You can stop right there. Sure, the blank page is challenging, but that's all. Heart surgery is terrifying; a blank page is just wood pulp. And besides, it's never really blank. Take comfort in the fact that you're never starting from zero. You're writing a memoir; you're already way ahead of aspiring novelists. You already know what happens; you know the characters, the plot, the outcome.

So in a sense, you've already started. Now all you have to do is keep going. In this chapter, the experts share how they managed to do that.

TO BEGIN

JONATHAN AMES: The best way to get going is to set a reasonable goal—I will write for one hour or I will write 300 words. By setting a reasonable goal it becomes less daunting to actually start. Also, the old Hemingway maxim of writing "one true sentence" can be very helpful. And then you try to write one more true sentence.

CAROLINE KRAUS: I know the right answer, which is to keep to a routine. I don't always succeed, but that's my goal, and for me it does work. I put myself in front of my notebook or laptop very early in the morning, before excuses set in. If nothing comes, I count it as a necessary part of the process nonetheless. I also make my writing environments as hospitable and easy as possible. I might transplant myself at the library for a change of view, and on good days I stop when there is still a little eagerness left to get going in the morning.

ELIZABETH GILBERT: Procrastination follows all of us, constantly, like a drug dealer offering you easy escape from reality. You can't fall for it, but it's difficult to resist. My problem as a writer isn't so much that I want to go live my life instead of writing; it's that I want to go lie down on the couch and eat cheese instead of writing.

Coaching yourself out of procrastination and getting back to work takes a giant, muscular, emotional effort, and the model I've always used to get myself working is to think of myself as a mule. Not an artist, but a mule. When it comes to putting a rough draft down on paper, my job is only this—to put my head down and plow from one end of the field (the page) to the next.

Part of the reason we procrastinate is because we judge our work too much—we write one sentence and think, "This is horrible," and then we quit in frustration. I think procrastination is not laziness, but disappointment. We wish we wrote better, and our inability to translate our dreams to the page can be crushing. But mules—when they are plowing fields—

do not stop, turn their heads, and contemplate whether or not they're doing a good job. When you're working on a first draft, you should no more look backwards at a sentence you've just written than a mule would wonder, "Gee, am I doing a good enough job plowing this field?" Later, when the first draft is finished, you can come back and mess around with your work, but not until you've got the field plowed completely—whether the job was done well or not. That model is the only way I've ever been able to get my work done. And when the inevitable voices rise, as I'm writing, saying, "This isn't good enough," I just answer back in my mule's voice: "That's not my problem. I was only hired to plow the field."

FRANK McCOURT: Scribble. That's what I tell all the writers I meet. Don't sit down to write a book, just start to scribble. Get your material down on paper. Then something will emerge. It will demand to be told. Then you get going. It's like a sculptor chipping away at a block of granite—something emerges.

You don't just sit and write. You have to scribble. You have to sketch if you're a painter. I think there's great value in scribbling. I scribbled for years, and I would listen to my high school students tell me, you should write a book, you should write a book. I always had the itch to write; I didn't have the itch to write a memoir until my students started telling me to.

I didn't procrastinate. Once I started *Angela's Ashes*, I was finished in thirteen months. *'Tis* took a little longer. *Teacher Man* took the longest. It was harder to write about teaching than about a miserable childhood.

STEPHEN ELLIOTT: I don't always, but I usually try to write first thing in the morning, before I do anything else like brush my teeth or take a shower.

A.J. JACOBS: I like to be very strict with myself. I told myself that I had to write at least 500 words a day, even if those words were all crap and would be rewritten the next day. It was a good motivator. Especially if you're scared of yourself, which I am. Who knows what I'm capable of doing if I don't follow my orders.

ISHMAEL BEAH: I wrote the first draft of my book while in college. With the help of Professor Dan Choan at Oberlin, I was able to have a schedule. Twice a week I met with him to submit a number of pages and to go over the previous submission. At first it was difficult because of the subject matter, but once I got going, the discipline to sit down and write improved.

MAXINE HONG KINGSTON: I always begin writing by jotting down notes about feelings and happenings which matter a lot to me. I am gathering clay. Then in about twenty drafts, shape and form become clear. An emotion, an image, a sound takes its place in a scene. A scene is the basic unit of drama. Write a series of scenes, connect them with transitions—voilà! You have your book. For me, this process works writing both fiction and nonfiction.

ANTHONY SWOFFORD: Even limericks induce procrastination. At least in me. Wake up. Drink coffee. Write. Ignore phone, ignore email, ignore world. It will all be there when you are done. Just don't ignore your lovers for too long. They might not stick around.

SARAH VOWELL: I've never in my life written something just for the heck of writing. I've only ever written for school or money. And the thing term papers, magazine articles, and books have in common that I so desperately need is a deadline.

JAMES MCMANUS: Writing is my job, and I go to my desk every day around 10 a.m., whether I'm writing fiction, the history of poker, or anything else. If I was working on a purely personal memoir, I'd do the same thing, but I think it might be harder having all that "freedom." I'm much more productive when I have tasks to complete: this week, for example, I'm summarizing the kinds of poker played during the Civil War. Once I've kitchen-sinked everything I've ever found out in books and online, the task becomes rearranging that information in a more and more natural way, writing better and clearer sentences, then moving on to the next task.

JANICE ERLBAUM: I didn't have any problems with procrastination; I was very motivated to tell my story. The only problem I had in getting started was where to begin. People say to "begin at the beginning," but what does that mean? Starting at birth? It's rarely a good idea to start at birth—babies are boring narrators. So you start wherever you can, with whatever piece of the story demands to be told first. You can go back and write the "beginning" later.

BETH LISICK: I enjoy the old-fashioned threat of a looming deadline.

RACHEL HOWARD: Well, I'm a person who likes to get things done—I'm just not much of a procrastinator, because I hate living with the stress of thinking there's work to take care of. But one thing that helped was to make the memoir a treat, a break from my "drudge" work of journalism. So I put my chapter drafts on a disk, and took them into my desk at the *San Francisco Examiner*, where I was a reporter. And when I finished an *Examiner* story, or wanted to put off finishing one that wasn't on deadline, I'd bring my memoir chapter up on the screen and let my bosses think I was writing dance reviews and such when I was really working on my book. This also taught me that I didn't need to set aside hours upon hours to make progress—I'd see a passage lock into form, or finally find the solution to structuring a certain scene while picking through it sentence-by-sentence in that way that you do when you've only got twenty minutes here, fifteen minutes there.

TANYA SHAFFER: When I returned from West Africa, the thoughts/feelings/impressions were so strong that I had to get them out just to clear some space in my head. Putting them on paper was a way of spending time with them while simultaneously freeing myself from them. I think for others who feel compelled to write a memoir of some period of their life it might work the same way. Write about what you have to get out.

STEVE ALMOND: I procrastinate with the best of them. But in the end I wind up feeling guilty if I don't write, like I'm wasting my precious time on earth. So it's mostly guilt that gets me going. It also helps if you write only about things that matter to you deeply. If there's no energy coming off the material, forget it.

AZADEH MOAVENI: I read Anne Lamott's *Bird by Bird*, and trained myself to sit in front of the computer a certain number of hours a day, simply as discipline. I think the process of sitting there is incredibly important, because you're not going to break through a slump unless you put in the hours and endure the slump in its entirety.

DAVID RAKOFF: All I do is procrastinate. Snacking, napping, phone calls, self-abuse. *Anything* but work. I respond well to deadlines, myself. Pressure and fear are my favorite engines. Virtually the only ones that work for me. What got me going initially was the terror that I was settling into a quietly desperate yet all-too comfortable life as The Funniest Guy in the Office. (Plus thousands of dollars and well over a decade's worth of psychotherapy.)

ON WARM-UP EXERCISES

ELIZABETH GILBERT: I don't know how you can warm up into writing except by writing. You have to write your way through the awkward beginnings until you find your voice. I find one of the most ridiculous moments in life to be that moment when you sit down at 9 a.m. on a Tuesday and begin writing a book. There it is. The first blank page vs.

your desire to create an entire book. It's crazy. How are you going to make *this* into *that*? You just have to start writing. Start even in mid-sentence ("and then I said to her ..."). Just get some words down.

The first few pages, or sometimes even chapters, of a new writing project are what I call The Runway—the airplane of your energies has to taxi down that runway, picking up speed before the prose can really start to fly. Don't worry too much about The Runway—you can always erase it later. It's flat and made of tar and it's boring, but you need to begin there, in order to get your speed, and then reach for your altitude.

TANYA SHAFFER: I often warm up with periods of free-writing, either about the topic I'm working on, or just about my day. Anything to get my hands and brain moving.

STEPHEN ELLIOTT: I used to write a letter to my girlfriend first. Then, when the letter was done (this was before email was big) I would start drinking coffee and begin to write.

ANTHONY SWOFFORD: Yoga. And some days I start by reading in other books I admire, a chapter here, a page there. I'll simply scour my bookshelves, read from ten or even twenty books, to remind myself that it can be done, and must.

JONATHAN AMES: Coffee. Email. Internet backgammon.

ISHMAEL BEAH: I played soccer and went for walks. I believe that writing also requires a significant amount of loneliness, so I tried to be alone for quite some time before starting to write.

NICK FLYNN: I do more of a daily writing practice, where I write for an hour in a notebook, usually generating five pages. If I'm working on a longer project I do the same practice, only steer the writing toward that project, that container. As Thich Nhat Hanh says about Buddha, "He already had the water, he just had to discover jars."

JANICE ERLBAUM: I didn't do warm-up exercises, but I did start by writing on themes. I wrote one piece called "Near-Death Experiences," which was all about the times where I felt like my life was in imminent peril. Then I wrote another one called "My Mother's Boyfriends" I followed that one up with "Public Break Ups." Writing on themes helped me to generate a lot of stories about my life, and to see the connections between them.

JAMES MCMANUS: I read *The New York Times* while eating breakfast, then take a cup of coffee into my office. I answer the phone for almost no one, eat lunch at my desk, and try to put in a good six or seven hours.

DAVID RAKOFF: I try to keep a diary, with only intermittent success, the thinking being not that I can use it later for material but rather that if I can prime the pump with a thousand words in the morning, then I can go on and write more stuff. Sadly, more often than not, I then just let myself off the hook and go eat some chips (Kettle Krinkle Cut Salt and Black Pepper. Beyond sublime).

FIROOZEH DUMAS: I work better in neat environments so I try to keep my desk clean.

RACHEL HOWARD: I would dip into a few pages of a memoir I admired—Tobias Wolff's *This Boy's Life* or Alexandra Fuller's *Don't Let's Go to the Dogs Tonight*—to get rolling.

I found it very helpful to begin a new chapter in a notebook, longhand, so that I would not be so given to prematurely editing myself. I would then transfer it onto the computer screen and pick up from there once I was on a roll.

I also like to sketch chapter outlines in my notebook, and find them comforting even if they turn out to be all wrong in the end.

LAURA FRASER: A lot of what I write starting out is what I call "throat-clearing." You have to write a bunch of stuff before you get to the real goods. So you go back and toss and edit.

A.J. JACOBS: Well, if you're not doing it already, start keeping a diary. And make it detailed. Not just emotions and sweeping statements, but what you ate, what you wore, snippets of conversation, the humidity level, fingernail length, etc. The more concrete the better. At least if you're looking to write about it later in a book. You won't use all of it, but it's so great to have.

DAN KENNEDY: I never really wait for inspiration to strike. I mean, I think I used to until I figured out that I'd been waiting for three years. Show up. Get some coffee or whatever, but first and foremost, show up.

IF YOU DON'T KNOW WHERE TO BEGIN

SARAH VOWELL: Read. Or a more accurate word might be "peruse." One simple way I've used to get historical story ideas was flipping through travel guidebooks. That's an easy way to discover local heroes, forgotten battlefields, scientific discoverers, etc. Also, of course, the newspaper. One of my favorite scenes in all cinema is the one in *Capote* when Truman Capote cuts out the tiny article from *The New York Times* about a murdered family in Kansas that would set him on the path to *In Cold Blood*. Finding the next thing to write about is almost as joyful a relief as finishing writing said thing.

BETH LISICK: Definitely start with the stuff that is the most fun for you to write. Pick a memorable scene, an interesting conversation, and then let the creative rivers flow where they will. You will eventually get to the hard parts, but make it easy on yourself at first. It has to be an enjoyable thing for you to do.

PAUL COLLINS: Begin with the preparation, and not with the writing. Take notes. Keep a journal but don't be afraid to ignore it, because what was important to you then may not be important to you now. Ask friends for your old letters: you will be alarmed and perturbed by who you were compared to who you *thought* you were. Read old newspapers from back then. Go back to old locations and take notes on the physical details. Research your own life the way you'd research anyone else's.

CAROLINE KRAUS: It depends on the story, but in my case I chose to begin at the lowest, most desperate point for the main character. This was a place that provoked the most questions and supplied the most tension and momentum.

JULIA SCHEERES: Start by writing down the pivotal events in your life. Pick one and describe it cinematically. Paint a picture with words. Then move onto the next. Write them chronologically, or in any order you'd like. That'll get the juices flowing. Then connect these events by reflecting on them and their significance—the musing part.

PHILLIP LOPATE: Begin with the piece or image of the past you see most clearly, and start describing it.

ISHMAEL BEAH: The general tendency is to start with perfect sentences, paragraphs, etc. Just start anywhere and the rest will come.

JONATHAN AMES: Start at the beginning of the most painful incident of your life, what lead to the moment of great pain, and what followed.

SEAN WILSEY: Write about something you really care about. I started by writing a book about alternative education, which I thought had a broader appeal. And then I ended up backing into the whole memoir thing, in order to explain how I'd arrived at an experimental school. It just exploded from there.

DAVID RAKOFF: I guess I would start with random memories, no matter how mundane. The artist Joe Brainard's book, *I Remember*, is simply a list of details. Some are weighty, some light as air, but the cumulative effect is so poetic and beautiful and unbelievably moving. It's really an absolute classic and a perfect exercise to start with.

FIROOZEH DUMAS: You can begin any place you want. You can always go back and write about something that happened earlier. You don't have to write in chronological order. Just write.

ELIZABETH GILBERT: Begin by deciding exactly who you are writing to. By this, I don't mean: "I'm writing to women between the ages of nineteen and twenty-nine," or "I'm writing to everyone who has ever lost a loved one from cancer." What I mean is—pick one, single person in this world, and tell your story directly to that person as though you are sitting across from them. If you don't do this, you story has no direct personal voice, and wanders and fluctuates from page to page, speaking into a meaningless vacuum.

Therefore, every time I've written anything—be it novel, memoir, or magazine article—I have waited to begin writing until I settle on the one person I'm telling my story to. It isn't the same person every time; I try to pick the person who would be most interested in this particular topic. I ask myself, "Would Andrew want to know about this? Would Sheryl?" Once you pick your reader—your one, single reader—never let them out of your sight. Keep that person in the room with you (mentally, that is) the whole time you're writing—even speak aloud to that person, asking, "Are you following me here? Is this getting boring? Am I explaining too much? Would you like to hear a funnier story now?"

I wrote *Eat, Pray, Love* entirely to my friend Darcey Steinke, who is also a writer whom I much admire. Like me, she'd been through divorce, depression, and a serious spiritual journey—she was the person I thought would be most interested in my story. And she's smart, so I tried to write at her level. And she's funny, so I tried to keep her entertained. When I would get stuck, I'd just write, "Dear Darcey—I'm getting bored here. What should I tell you about today?" and the story would un-stick. In the end, what happens when you write like this is that perfect strangers will read your work later, and come up to you and say, "I felt like you were talking directly to me."

DAN KENNEDY: You don't need to know where. Start with the middle if you want to, because you're going to revise the whole damn thing five times anyway, so don't hold yourself to any rules about where to start. For all you know the beginning's going to wind up being the end.

TANYA SHAFFER: Take a workshop where you're expected to turn things in. Make sure you have to pay your hard-earned money for it, so you value it. Nothing like a deadline to get things out of your head and onto the page.

STEVE ALMOND: Just begin. Don't put so much pressure on yourself. It's just a draft. Try to remember that any time spent at the keyboard is time in heaven. (True.)

MATTHUE ROTH: Talk about today. Talk about your first memory. Pick one instant in your life, and start from there. Record yourself talking, and then take notes as you play it back. Listen to yourself in a conversation with your best friend. Take the best stories from there, and build them up.

ALISON SMITH: There's no perfect place to begin. You don't have to know your opening scene or the structure of your book or the overarching theme before you start. In fact if you wait till you've got it all figured out you may never begin. For me, writing is a way of thinking. I don't know what I'm writing about till I am in the middle of it. That is the joy of writing. It's also the most frightening thing about it. Because there's no guarantee that you'll figure it out, that you'll write a good book, that you'll ever finish it. But one thing I know for sure: if you don't start, you definitely won't finish.

ON FALSE STARTS

JANICE ERLBAUM: The whole first draft of my book could be considered a "false start," but I prefer to think of it as a "first draft." It was certainly painful to write 300 pages and have them rejected by agents and editors—I was so frustrated and dejected, I didn't know how I was going to start over from scratch. But I don't think I could have written the second version of the book without having written the first. The first draft taught me the discipline of writing five days a week, it taught me how to look for and articulate the right word or phrase or feeling, and it got me to face a lot of emotionally painful material. All that practice made me a better writer, and helped me with the second draft of the book. It definitely was not a waste of time.

ALISON SMITH: It took six years and eighteen drafts to write *Name All the Animals*. It is the hardest thing I have ever willingly signed up for in my life. When I started it in 1996, I was quite naïve. I had no idea what writing a memoir would entail. And I made every mistake in the book. My first draft was 800 pages long and I rarely appeared in it! Leaving yourself out of your own life story is quite an oversight. The book opens in 1984, the summer my brother died in a car accident. He was eighteen that summer and just about to leave for college when he died. I was fifteen. I've thought a lot about why it was so hard to put myself into this story.

I think I struggled so because sibling grief is overlooked in our culture. When a child dies, we look to the parents. They are center stage in the tragedy. If siblings are noticed at all, it is only as an extension of the parents. They are told that they must make up for the lost child, they must look after their parents. I really bought into this line of thinking. When I started to write the book, I thought that I would write the story of my parents' lives, of everything they lost when Roy died. I thought that was the authentic family experience. It took me quite some time to realize that the sister's story was a very important story as well.

FIROOZEH DUMAS: Years before I started writing my book, I applied to a writing program twice and got rejected. I wrote a fiction story for my application that I recently re-read. It was okay but not great. Then years later, I started writing nonfiction for my kids and everything clicked. I found my voice right away and I had so much fun. I still have fun when I write. That's an important detail for me. I don't do misery well.

RACHEL HOWARD: I wrote short stories about my sociopath heroin addict stepfather first, and also about my depression and breakdown at age twenty. Then I thought I would write about my father's murder as a novel. That wouldn't work, because the details of his death were so bizarre, and I wasn't willing to change any details because what I was trying to do was make sense of them.

Finally I decided I was writing a memoir, and my first attempts at chapters were meandering remembrances of life with my dad just before he died. Some of this material did end up getting massaged into something useful later, though. But my real breakthrough came the night I sat down to write everything I could remember about waking up in that dark house at 3:30 in the morning and seeing that my father had just been stabbed. It was terrifying— I was literally looking over my shoulder, feeling someone might stab me as I wrote it. When I was done I knew I could handle whatever memories writing this book might bring up, and I no longer had to tiptoe around "dangerous" material.

NICK FLYNN: Many, many false starts, which seem essential to an honest process of discovery, to me. I had no idea what shape it would take when I began it, if it would be a poem, or poems, or something else.

JONATHAN AMES: I've had numerous false starts, both in nonfiction and fiction. In some box, I have half a novel that I false-started about seventeen years ago, worked on it for a year. I don't really recall what's in it ... And with essays and short stories, nearly every published piece probably had a false start.

CAROLINE KRAUS: I had many false starts. I couldn't get over the audacity of devoting a whole book to me. But when I began to see it as a book about attachment and loss, I was able to separate myself from the story. I felt more like a character in a common story.

Chapter IV

LINES, CURVES, AND TANGENTS

Shaping your story

Memoirs come in as many different shapes as the people who write them. Some are long and dense, others short and spare. They are explicit, mysterious, funny, sober. Some are told backwards and some skip around. Several have been written as cookbooks, others as how-tos. One was written as an encyclopedia. Any format can work, and yours might be something altogether new.

Don't be disheartened if it takes multiple, widely varying drafts. Many successful memoirs started out as something else entirely. Some were bad novels, some were plays, some were journals or emails. Some were written in overwrought language that would dissuade any reader; others, in straight reportorial style that strip-mined all emotion. Then they got edited, fixed, published. The point is that this is a process, and your first draft will not be your last. It shouldn't be, anyway. The vast majority of every book that's ever been, has at one time or another been an incredible mess. It's part of the getting-there, and the tributaries you find yourself along the way will, believe it or not, make the book better. You'll find the right words. Or maybe the words-only format is the wrong medium entirely for your memoir. Maybe it should be a graphic novel. If so, Art Spiegelman and Ellen Forney are here with advice and tips.

In this chapter writers discuss the pros and pitfalls of different memoir formats, sharing how they find the blueprints that work for them.

ON FINDING A SHAPE FOR THE STORY

AMY KROUSE ROSENTHAL: I had spent months and months researching nonfiction formats. I knew that I didn't have a traditional life story to tell, that I had no business writing a major autobiography or straight-up memoir. This was clear, this I knew. And I had a definite sense of the kind of stuff I wanted to write about, the kind of stuff I already was writing about ... and so the quest became: What kind of vessel will hold this material?

Just as it is always the case when you can't find your keys, and that you find them in the last place you look, I stumbled upon my solution only after looking in every other nook and cranny. It finally occurred to me one day to take a look at the encyclopedia, to re-examine it, just for the sake of completing my research. I thought, okay, the encyclopedia is the ultimate king form of nonfiction. I randomly grabbed a volume off my shelf and threw it on my bed to look at that night before falling asleep. The volume I had chosen was "E." So later that night, I started paging through it. I remember reading Einstein's entry, which, of course, was fascinating and cool.

Soon enough, I found myself at the entry for the actual encyclopedia, which itself was interesting to me, reading about the encyclopedia in an encyclopedia. I read about its history, creation, different incarnations, its unique format and devices. I hadn't really delved into an encyclopedia since college, but it felt comfortable returning, that whole world of "see also's" and graphic devices (charts, etc.) and concise entries that I had grown up with as a kid/student. After a short while, and in a sudden flash, it hit me: "This is it, this is the vessel." I knew it then: "I am going to write a personal encyclopedia. That is the exact right—the only right—format. This is the book I have actually been writing all along, but I just didn't know it ..."

ANTHONY SWOFFORD: I let memory guide me, and memory, at least mine, works in rather nonlinear fashion, so that images from the present propel me into images of the past. I also let themes guide me, and link periods of narrative thematically and imagistically. Of course, all of this—themes and images—is about meaning. The structure of the book is the meaning of the book. Not what, but how. One finds the proper structure by writing and failing and writing and failing and one day writing and discovering. There is no trick, only that old bugaboo, work.

JAMES MCMANUS: Chronology is your friend. You can always move around in time, pause much longer at one place than another, but the best basic shape is usually Time A through Time Z.

ISHMAEL BEAH: I first wrote my story out chronologically and then through editing, I realized that the experience itself had a structure. For example, during my running from the war, I thought a lot about how life was before the madness, and at the rehabilitation center, I came to fully face the difficult memories that I had put at bay while in the army. My advice would be to first write as much as you can, and the structure will come about once you have much of the story on the page.

PAUL COLLINS: Segues are the canary in the memoirist's coal mine. If you can't fashion meaningful transitions, it might be because there aren't any—and in that case, essays make more sense for expressing your experiences. But working around a chronology is intrinsically power-ful because that is how we experience out lives: not as essays, but as a cyclical narrative with variations. Life resembles an almanac a lot more than it resembles a sermon.

ART SPIEGELMAN: That's the challenge I handle best. More than rendering figures or outlining draft after draft, the finding of form is exactly what I like to do. It's satisfying. I don't do crossword puzzles but I suspect it has some of the same pleasures. That's the part I like. Everything else is just making it manifest. What I like about comics is you're dealing literally with shapes. Ultimately, the page is the shape that you've given to the visual paragraph that you're writing.

TOBIAS WOLFF: I had told many of the stories that appear in *In This Boy's Life* over the years. In the natural course of things, as you tell stories about the past, the stories themselves begin to shape the memory. Perhaps in the case of that book there was a natural tendency on my part to see the narrative as progressing through a series of stories, a number of narratives that made a larger story.

FRANK MCCOURT: I told the story chronologically, writing about whatever was urgent, or somehow cast light on the situation. There were parts and moments in my life which were very tragic and sad, and yet there was humor. There was no great plan. I went from moment to moment, from day to day, and had no big outline.

JONATHAN AMES: Personally, I love to work chronologically, in a linear fashion. That's not for everybody, but that's how my mind works and, too, it represents how the event, how the life itself, unfolded. But that's not necessarily the approach for everybody.

I find, though, that *time* creates plot and tension—that relaying, directly, how an event unfolded—with some tangents, flashbacks, explanations—just naturally builds suspense. The old beginning, middle, and end structure. I'm stuck on it, for better or worse. It worked nicely, though, for Shakespeare, so what the heck ...

DAN KENNEDY: I think a lot of people make the mistake of thinking it's all up to them. The work itself will start to take on shape and structure as it becomes its own thing, dictating a lot of this.

The whole thing's bigger than you, you know, so you can relieve yourself of the burden of thinking you're in control of it. If you think you're driving, you're wrong. You're the passenger. As a matter of fact, you're not even riding shotgun—you're in the back seat, man. Come to think of it, you don't even get to decide if the windows are up or the air conditioning's on, that's how much of a passenger you are in this thing. That's a truth and a trick.

JANICE ERLBAUM: I suggest that a writer starts by getting through the first draft any way they can—in chronological order or out of it, grouping stories based on themes or subjects—however the material comes out, great. Then look at it, and see if there's any way to make it a straight chronological narrative—readers tend to like those—or if there's some other organic organizational principle that suggests itself to you. Then rearrange your material accordingly, and start that second draft.

STEPHEN ELLIOTT: Things like the shape present themselves later, usually. At least for me.

NICK HORNBY: I had been writing a lot of journalism in the two years leading up to *Fever Pitch*, mostly eight-hundred-word book reviews. My memoir was my first book, and the prospect of filling it up was pretty daunting, so when I hit on the idea of these game reports [each of them around 800 words], it was perfect for me—I was writing to a length that I knew I could handle.

AZADEH MOAVENI: This is the really tough part. I think I attempted to organize around both themes and chronology, which involved a fair amount of creative nipping and tucking. I think that unless you're Princess Diana (about whom everything is automatically interesting, even brands of toilet paper) or Nabokov (whose memoir is stylized and exists outside the genre), you have to carry the double burden of moving your narrative along chronologically, and just allowing your themes to emerge naturally. This task of entertaining with a story and illuminating with carefully ordered insight is formidable, and I found that huge pieces of poster board with a timeline for the chronology and big circles for themes helped me map out my story.

STEVE ALMOND: I'm the wrong person to ask. *Candyfreak* is a big, fat mess. Then again, I like that it's a big, fat mess. I'm not big on imposing structure. The prose should be lucid, the ideas organized.

I'm not sure the form matters so much to readers. They just want a good story to hook into.

RACHEL HOWARD: From the start I wanted it to be a continuous narrative, because the story of my father's murder felt fragmented. It felt like so many pieces were missing from what I knew, and my drive was to make it whole. Interestingly, though, I am now working on what I hope will become a second memoir. It's about my marriage, and I've gone back and forth between shorter, self-contained essays and a vision for a full book-length arc. Then finally I found the thread that tied all the story lines together: my obsession with a particular place as a fantasy home. Sometimes the "subject" you think you're writing about is really just the "symptom" of a deeper story that taps into more universal desires—it's the surface story, not the underlying drive.

MATTHUE ROTH: For the most part, the structure will find itself. That isn't to say that you don't have to give it little tweaks ... and, sometimes, big tweaks. The key is to start off talking about just one thing—one event, one person, or one day, something like that. Let the other elements naturally work their way in. Don't barrage the reader with too much information, of course; but once you let the story tell itself, the plot will fall into place. If only because, sooner or later, people *do* things. Sometimes amazing things, mostly stupid things, but things that other people want to hear about.

A.J. JACOBS: I love a predetermined structure. Some sort of architecture on which I can hang my words. I organized *The Know-It-All* alphabetically: chapter A, chapter B, etc. That was nice. I wish I could write all my books alphabetically. But sadly, that might get repetitive. Even if you do something nutty and go with reverse alphabetical for some of them. The alphabet is such a clear set of landmarks, it let me weave together a lot of strands that otherwise might have gotten confusing—namely, the facts from the encyclopedia, stuff about my childhood, and the effect massive knowledge intake had on my life.

For my second book, I chose to structure it by leading each mini-chapter with a Bible quote. It served the same purpose as the alphabet. So I say, whenever possible, find a pre-existing structure you can co-opt for your own purposes.

ALISON SMITH: That first massive draft contained everything from my great-great grandparents' emigration from Denmark to what my mother wore to her high school graduation. It was just missing one necessary ingredient: a point of view. It took me a long time to figure out that just about the only thing you've got going for you as a memoirist is your point of view. There are a lot of ways to tell the story of what happened to my family. But there's only one point of view I have a right to, and that is my own. Once I got a grasp of that tricky concept, I realized that the whole book had to be organized around my experience of grief, my coming-of-age, my discovery. That became the organizing principle—so even though most of the characters know how my brother died by the end of chapter two, the reader does not find out until I find out, two years later, halfway through the book.

FIROOZEH DUMAS: Write what you enjoy reading. I love reading first-person stories that are between three and ten pages long. That's what I write.

I consider my books like a photo album. I try to put my photos and stories in order but there are gaps and not everything has to be covered. I don't mind if the reader is left with some questions. My goal is to explain certain parts of my life, but not everything. I just make sure that each story makes sense, and stands alone.

HOW TO CONTROL THE TIMELINE

ART SPIEGELMAN: You make an outline, and then you violate it and rework and rework. I have to start with some kind of fairly delineated trajectory of what happened when.

Years ago, when I did *Maus*, I was wondering if I should deal with my father's story as stream-of-consciousness (he didn't stick to a chronology when he told me his life story, but proceeded through an association of ideas, and in some ways I was thinking the most honest thing to do was to live with that as the flow). And then I realized if I did I would still be working with some arbitrary construction, and that impeded understanding a history already too difficult to comprehend.

The basic template of temporal progression always gets violated; it's impossible to have a complete thought. Still, having that as the touchstone is necessary. In *Maus* I was desperately trying to stay in temporal order, even though the story wasn't coming to me that way.

You have to find a way of indicating the chronology without allowing it to have final say. Because ultimately, all of this is an art of indication.

JAMES MCMANUS: "Narrative slop," Lorrie Moore calls what we're faced with. That's the task, to find the right order for every issue, passage, phrase, and word. It ain't easy, so if you're suffering while trying to do it, know that every writer, no matter how famous, is in exactly the same boat. We also have to decide whether an issue or term should be defined parenthetically now or later on; or occur two scenes earlier, where it may be less awkward. Stick the explanatory scene into three or four places and see where it works best.

ELIZABETH GILBERT: This was easier for me than it might have been for others, because my book was about a journey that took place within a very recognizable narrative structure—I traveled for a year, to three countries, looking for something specific in each place. In other words,

I lived my life for one year as though it were a book, divided into three sections, filled with chapters and scenes of my experiences.

My journey was laid out like a book, probably because I'm an author and I know what makes a good story. Writing it down later was simple (well, not simple ... but *simpler*) because the structure was already all there. Beginning, middle, end, contained timeline, motivation ... I think it would be much harder to write about something more vague, like "my childhood," or "my parents." But to chronicle a year's journey? There's a clear order to it, automatically.

ANTHONY SWOFFORD: The controlling factor of all memoirs should be the battle between narrative life and real life. Narrative life, the life of the book, must always win. This will fix pesky chronology problems. Your life is less important than your book.

FRANK McCOURT: I wrote *Angela's Ashes* just off the cuff. There was no control. Whatever came to me, just came to me. You know the way a child tugs at a skirt, saying listen, listen. These things tugged at me, saying tell me, tell me. And there was the element of enjoyment. There are things you get no pleasure writing about, but things you like to write about, whether they're sad or funny.

DAN KENNEDY: You can shrink the timeline to save the reader the pain of a chapter that would be just, you know, five thousand words about how you watched TV for a year and worked at your day job and wondered what was next. But that's about the only liberty I take with timelines. If on page 95 you're living in San Francisco, and technically it took another three uneventful years until you moved to Spain, well, I'd recommend putting the beginning of the Spain chapter on page 96 and maybe skipping the boring stuff where you're watching TV and working a day job and going, "Someday I think I'd like to move to Spain." But if you were in Spain for three weeks, don't say you were there for three years.

JANICE ERLBAUM: Always let your reader know what time of year you're taking about, and which year, if possible. Part of the background setting of your book should include the seasons, the weather, the holidays, or important events that are occurring around you. Adding phrases like "two weeks later" or "the following school year" will always help your readers stay with your timeline. If you skip around in time, date your chapters—"Chapter Six: Minor Tragedies (1987)."

CAROLINE KRAUS: I taped a timeline up near my desk, and I used it when I needed to, but I didn't let that interrupt the creative part of writing. I knew I could always go back and check myself, so I tried not to make those details important until after the pages were done.

AZADEH MOAVENI: To some extent, I think most memoirists take a certain liberty with time. For example, if a certain incident happened chronologically before another, but for the purposes of your story you want to imply it happened later, there are descriptive crutches that can help. You can describe a few events that happened within a season, for example, rather than providing a blow-by-blow account with references to specific months.

DAVID MATTHEWS: Every event had to be tied to a certain theme; for me, that theme was identity. So if there was an event that was interesting, or funny, or dramatic, but didn't fit the larger theme—it didn't make the story. After deciding on theme, it was easy to order the events in my life which illustrated that theme. Theme gave me the guideposts for what to put in, but just as importantly, what to leave out.

STEVE ALMOND: Just stick to the most important events and cut the B material. And don't wrinkle the chronology, if you can avoid it. It just confuses the reader. And my number one rule is: Never confuse the reader.

PAUL COLLINS: I try not to break with the chronology of actual events, as tempting as it may be, because part of the power of memoir is that the reader is walking along alongside you and discovering things as you did. If you break out of the narration, the reader loses that sense of discovery, and you diminish the tension of the book. A memoirist needs to be patient, and not give themselves away too quickly.

RACHEL HOWARD: Oh boy, I wish I'd had a strategy instead of pure trial-and-error. In general, though: write from *scenes*. Be in the moment, even if the memory is so indistinct or fragmented that you can do that only for a few paragraphs at a time. Timeline is easily signposted later, with a sentence of clarification here, a "this was six months after such-and-such" there.

Because my memories were fragmented, though, I had to constantly flesh out timelines for my own reference in my notebooks. Sometimes this revealed interesting things—for instance, I'd always thought I'd only lived with my father for one summer, when in fact when he was killed we were starting summer number two—and sometimes realizing these things became part of the material of the book. I had tried to forget the fact of that earlier summer for a reason.

NICK FLYNN: I write out what I remember first, which will likely reveal some confusion in the actual chronology, when you get around to researching what it actually was. But this confusion, this misremembering, is what is interesting. That said, the actual chronology is vitally important. For example, I eventually discovered that the two major stretches of jail, then prison time, my father did came after his mother died, and then after his father died. By finding that out, the crimes he committed that led him to prison or jail could be read as reactions to grief, perhaps, and thereby allowed me an insight I wouldn't have otherwise had. And most insights, it seems, lead to compassion, which is the goal of a memoir, as far as I can tell.

TAMIM ANSARY: I wasn't aware of it, and that's because I didn't think in terms of chronology that much. I thought in terms of episodes and themes. Chronology is more if you're writing something that's like a biography. To me, when I'm at a party, I really enjoy telling stories and talking to people. If I'm talking to someone and I remember something I want to tell them about, I don't have any trouble with chronology. The moment I start talking I'm pointed to the effect I want to have. It's not about chronology. It's about moving toward your end point. I think that's true of all writing in a way.

One of the things I'm obsessed with is the profluence of a story—the sense that it's moving forward. A lot of people mistakenly think of that in terms of plot. I think what keeps a story moving forward is purpose. In stories that interest me, I have the sense from the start that they're going someplace. With memoir, it's the same—you're going someplace.

FINDING THE NARRATIVE
ARC IN YOUR LIFE

TOBIAS WOLFF: Looking back on my life, I saw a certain narrative shape. That may be because I was looking back on it.

In the course of writing the book, memories came to me that displaced others. So the shape of the story changed as I was writing it. You can't be confident that the memoir you set out to write is the one you will write. You should, in fact, discover things that will upset your original design.

SEAN WILSEY: Narrative isn't something you impose upon the story—it actually exists. When the events are happening, you might not see that. But with enough time and distance, you do start to have a real sense of the narrative of your life. You realize, I did *this* because of *this*.

My advice to the aspiring memoirist is: wait. Wait until you feel that you've achieved a real understanding of events you want to write about. Only then do those events start to acquire a narrative. The understanding comes with time and a genuine desire to understand. I think a lot of people do the opposite, and write a memoir to understand things, but that just isn't my style.

FRANK McCOURT: I think there are moments in your life that are hot and there are moments that are cold, and you want to get those hot moments, like a child dying, or your first communion, or your confirmation, or your first day of school, last day in school, all of that, these significant moments. Sometimes you remember things that you previously considered insignificant. There's hardly any moment that's insignificant if you start thinking about it.

LAURA FRASER: You have to remember that it's a story, and has to have the ingredients of a story: character development, setting the stage, conflicts and stakes along the way, some sort of climax or epiphany, and then a resolution. Pretend it's not about you, it's a novel.

ISHMAEL BEAH: I believe that once you know what you want to convey from your life's experiences, you can then select moments or instances of those experiences to support the overall message of your book or whatever questions you want to raise.

STEPHEN ELLIOTT: I think Elmore Leonard said something like: I just write down everything and then I get rid of the boring parts.

FIROOZEH DUMAS: I just write short stories and trust that together, they make some kind of cohesive quilt. Some readers really like the way my book is not really "organized." Others dislike it for the same reason. You just have to do what feels right for your story and let go.

DAVID MATTHEWS: The spine, or heart of my book was the theme of identity, so every chapter had to flow from that. How to build the story is a matter of having a question—in my book, "What is identity?"— and then setting out to answer that question over the course of the book. The trick is, to highlight the question with anecdotes that probe the question—but delay the answer. Get the reader involved in the protagonist's life so that they're invested in solving the problem with the narrator, but keep 'em from the answers until the last possible moment—the end.

It's a tricky maneuver, but one that almost every movie and comic book uses. Comic books are a great way to get the hang of how to build tension over the course of a story. Flip to the last page of any comic book, and you'll find the you've got more questions on the last page than you had when you started. In a book, of course, you can answer those questions, but treat every chapter as a separate "comic book" to keep the reader turning the pages.

JANICE ERLBAUM: You find the "story of your life" by asking yourself this question: What did you want more than anything? Was it the love of your parents, or romantic love, or an end to abuse, or financial security, or self-esteem, or a puppy, or to be famous, or to stop being bulimic, or what? Then you go back and look at everything that happened that affected this goal—the things that made you want this goal in the first place, and the things that stood in your way of getting them, and everything you did to try to achieve your goal. This is the story: the pursuit of a goal. Even if you don't get your goal in the end, or you decide you don't want it anymore, the pursuit of a goal is the basis of a good life story.

AZADEH MOAVENI: I think you spend a lot of time writing all the feeling and content out of yourself, and then looking at it dispassionately on the screen. Once it's staring back at you from a computer, it is fairly easy to tell what you wrote simply because you needed to write it, and what you wrote that is meaningful to your book.

STEVE ALMOND: Focus on those moments that feel emotionally charged, that stay with you and sting. Don't waste your time on filler.

PAUL COLLINS: I always try to remind myself: I'm the only person who knows what's been left out. A reader doesn't know what a book was supposed to be or what it could have been—they only know what it is. So I'm unsentimental about junking anything that doesn't build the piece up, that won't contribute to the greater good of the piece. I might miss it, but the reader won't.

BETH LISICK: I don't think I was too successful at this. I just hoped that people would be entertained enough to want to follow me to the next chapter. Because it was episodic, I just cut out most of the mess and boring parts and went straight to the sex and car chases.

ANTHONY SWOFFORD: You build tension and plot by ignoring chronology. Also, more than fiction, memoir is about characters, people, and you rub them up against each other and they make story. Unless you were chasing spies or flying into space, you probably have lived a boring life.

TANYA SHAFFER: That's the gift writing gives us—it helps us give order to our disorderly lives. But in fact, we all have that impulse anyway. It's what we do when we tell the story of our life. We make it make sense in retrospect. I really feel that the best way to learn about how to tell a story is to tell it to your friends. Say it out loud and notice what you leave in and what you take out. If you don't have a chance to do that, at least pretend you're telling it to someone when you're writing.

We all have an inherent sense of what makes a good story. Listen to that inner knowledge. Include the moments that heighten the central drama and take out those that don't.

RACHEL HOWARD: I am a *huge* advocate for keeping journals, not only because you'll have written details to refresh your memory, should you choose to write about those events later, but because the regular practice of writing in a journal trains you to think of your life in terms of narrative shape. I've kept journals since age eighteen and write in my journal every two to four days. I think it's what's made me a memoirist. Trying to impose some shape on my life as it's happening gives me a reassuring sense that I am living out a coherent story—even if that story is my ongoing creation.

I feel like I can see various stories in my life overlapping—I'm at one place in the arc of the story of my divorce, at another in the arc of the story of my brother's Army service in Iraq, at another in the arc of the story of my relationship with my grandfather now that my grandmother has died. Once you start training yourself to see your life this way, it can be overwhelming—memoir material is everywhere.

It's also—not to get all self-help on you—hugely empowering to think of your life as an ongoing story, because when you do that you get to make choices about what happens next. You really are writing your own life.

THREE FORMS TO CONSIDER

If your memoir just isn't working as a straightforward, nonfiction, chronological narrative—or if you're the experimental type—you might want to try one of the following forms. The roman à clef, the graphic novel, and the essay all provide great storytelling opportunities that more traditional forms don't always permit. Read on to see if one of them might suit you.

I. THE ROMAN À CLEF

There are a lot of good reasons to consider writing your story as fiction instead of memoir. Maybe your life needs a little punching up to be a great book. Maybe you have a talent for exaggeration and an impatience for facts. Maybe you have litigious family members, or a history of prosecutable offenses. If so, you may want to consider writing your story as a roman à clef. But there are trade-offs; you're exchanging authenticity for freedom, emotional resonance for great drama. We asked our authors if they ever thought about writing their book as a novel instead.

LAURA FRASER: Yes, mainly because it was so personal.

FRANK MCCOURT: I tried and it didn't work. It seems false and forced, creating characters, but it was me and my family all the time. Nobody would believe it. Someone asked me once in San Francisco, "Why didn't you write a novel?" I said no one would believe it. They'd say I was exaggerating.

ISHMAEL BEAH: I just couldn't do it as a novel even though I thought about that many times as a way of avoiding to stand behind the intimate details of my life. The reason was simply that one of the most important purposes of the book was to put a human face to the story of children affected by war; a novel couldn't do that.

ELIZABETH GILBERT: Oh dear heavens, no. Why would I go through the huge effort to write a novel (what my friend Megan refers to as "a 300-page hair-shirt") when I could tell this already-existent true story, instead?

TANYA SHAFFER: Sometimes I wanted to. Things would come into my mind that would make the story more interesting but weren't strictly true, and I wished I could follow them. But since I'd already published many sections as nonfiction I decided to stick with that. I might write a novel next time, though, to give myself more freedom.

JANICE ERLBAUM: No. The truth is always stranger than fiction, and I think it's helpful to readers (especially young readers) to read about events and situations that a real person has lived through and overcome.

TAMIM ANSARY: I started out telling this story as a novel. I had a novel all written and my agent was about to sell it. Then 9/11 happened and my agent said I needed a nonfiction book. I looked at the novel and realized many scenes came directly from life. I was able to get at the story so much better by eliminating any fictional trappings.

GUS LEE: I fictionalized our family stories because I was afraid of my father's reaction. Although he could no longer threaten me physically, I still feared his bad opinion of me. When, at the age of ninety-one, he became terminally ill, he told me the stories that had remained unknown about our family in China. Those stories naturally relieved in me a lifelong tension with our past, and naturally became family nonfiction.

JULIA SCHEERES: No. I felt my true story was as dramatic as any fictive account and more powerful because it was true. I wanted to immortalize my brother in *Jesus Land*. It's an account of his life and struggles and of our relationship.

MATTHUE ROTH: For sure. Even when people ask today, I still want to tell them it's a novel, sometimes. But there are some things that you can't write using the novel voice. And if a memoir only has one thing going for it, it's the memoirist's voice ... you can always call it a novel when you're done. But when you're writing it, own it.

NICK HORNBY: There were lots of reasons [I wrote a memoir instead]. As a sports fan, I'm not particularly interested in fiction about pro sports. When I do read it, it seems phony to me; how come I've never heard of this team? I think fans are pretty literal-minded. I could still have written a novel about a real team and real games, but it would have felt like hiding. I wanted to say, "This is who I am, and this is who *we* are," and making it all up wasn't the point. Plus, having to stick to the facts was actually a comforting sort of discipline for a first-time author. If you can go anywhere and write about anything, how the hell do you know where to go? I'd left myself a trail I could follow, and I was grateful for it.

II. THE GRAPHIC NOVEL

Some of our very favorite memoirs are written in comic-strip form. Pictures and words play off each other in a way that's poignant and powerful and funny all at once. We asked some of our favorite graphic memoirists how they do what they do.

ART SPIEGELMAN: It's a complicated answer to a simple question. I can sort of write and I can sort of draw, so the solution has to exist somewhere between the two zones, and there's a lot of back and forth. In my more autobiographical pieces I start with a text of some form. Starting from the words, I have to look at the text to find the visual component later. I really do need some kind of visual anchor. There's got to be something visual to hang onto or it's just going to be talking heads for the next thirty pages, folks.

Some advice that I got from reading a writer named Marguerite Yourcenar was this: If you only deal with the personal the work is going to be incomplete. If you only deal with the social and political, the work is going to be incomplete. You really have to find where both things cross over to make a work worth making.

To do that, one has to have a very good editor in one's head, and then find a way to tie the editor up with an S&M ball gag long enough to get something done, and then untie him long enough to show you how to fix it.

ELLEN FORNEY: I teach comics at Cornish College of the Arts in Seattle, and I give my students this progression: Idea—Research—Script—Thumbnail—Good pencil—Ink/render—Scan/tweak—Reduce/reproduce. I make sure to say that it's not so neat as that reduction, that they'll hop around, and that it's important to edit every step of the way. But really, for the most part, I do follow that progression pretty closely.

Some comics come to me more visually, practically complete. Every once in a while I'll just spill out a story without knowing where it's going or how it will end. A few weeks ago, I woke up in the middle of the night with a complete one-page comic in my head—that's why I keep paper and a pen next to my bed. I wish that happened more often!

In deciding what to draw and what to write, I mostly try not to be redundant—except occasionally for humorous intent. ("Look, a shiny apple!" with a drawing of a shiny apple, vs. "It was so tempting, so forbidden," with the same image.) I usually try to keep the text to a minimum—if there's something in the text that I can show in a draw-ing, I'll opt for the drawing. On the other hand, I like words and I like writing, so my comics have a fair bit of text in them. You can get specific with text in a way that you can't with drawings. I guess it's pretty much just intuitive, weaving them together.

Advice for the aspiring graphic memoirist: Reading other auto-biographical comics might be helpful—I'd highly recommend *Fun Home*—but if you're comfortable with your own style, just take off and work hard and have fun. Ask yourself: What stories about your life do you tell your friends? The time you farted in front of the person you had a crush on? The big argument you had with your mother about hating Crest toothpaste, when you were six? Skinny-dipping in a neighbor's pool? It's a good bet those are the stories that you want to make into comics. Also, remember that even in an autobiographical story—shh, secret—you don't have to tell it *exactly* exactly like it happened. Nip, tuck, exaggerate—all fair in storytelling.

III. THE ESSAY

Many, if not most, memoirs begin as essays. It's such a manageable form: you relate an event in five or ten or twenty pages, and then you move on to the next one. Plus, chances are you're already an expert essay-writer. You had to write hundreds of essays in school; you have the structure down cold. We asked some of our favorite authors of memoir essays about their thoughts on the form.

DAVID RAKOFF: The essay form works for me because I cannot stop interjecting. What was that show (that I never once saw in my en-tire life), *Mystery Science Theater 3000*, I think it was called? Where the silhouettes in the darkened theater comment constantly on the action up on the screen? Well, such is my narcissism and near-crippling self-consciousness that I lack the ability to simply be quiet within myself and just have an experience without sullying it with my constant prodding, palpating, and general handling of it with my greasy little fingers.

What am I feeling about this right this very second. This reminds me of that joke/movie/time I blahblahblah! Everybody listen to me! (good for writing I suppose; for living ... well, the jury's out).

SARAH VOWELL: I think a good guideline for any kind of essayist is that he or she should try and tack some kind of idea onto his or her essay. A good essay has a good point.

PHILLIP LOPATE: I like the essay form because it's flexible and conversational, and has the potential to develop a bond of intimacy between reader and writer. I also find true life to be sufficiently amazing that I like to take it "neat" or as is. My advice is: a) be as honest as you can be; b) read widely and intensively in the genre; c) practice acquiring a polished literary style, with linguistic texture, syntactical variety, irony, and nuance.

Chapter V

METHODS FOR MOVEMENT

Schedules, bursts, and other structures and strictures

The first thing to know about the process of writing is that you spend most of your time not writing. There's the time spent researching and thinking, the time spent daydreaming and snacking, the time spent cleaning your desk as a procrastinatory tactic, the time spent watching CNN *(for background) and the time spent watching* Love and Death *(also background). For most people, the actual tapping-away-at-the-keyboard time is comparatively brief.*

That said, you do have to log some decent time at said keyboard. Most memoirists find it works best to park yourself there, hell or high water, for a few hours a day while you're trying to bang the thing out, but everybody's different. Some people need structured work hours while others work in bursts, some outline and others write free-form, some collaborate and others go it alone. Memoirs have been written under all conceivable conditions: in internment camps and office jobs, on Post-It notes and hundred-foot scrolls. Helen Keller wrote hers in Braille. Cerebral palsy sufferer Christy Brown could only scrawl, per the title of his memoir, with his left foot. After a stroke left everything but one eyelid completely paralyzed, Jean-Dominique Bauby managed to write his memoir, The Diving Bell and the Butterfly, *by blinking his left eyelid to choose each letter of the alphabet. We have reiterate this:* He wrote an entire book by blinking letters. *A busy schedule? A prehistoric computer? These are no challenges at all, no obstacles to the juggernaut that is your book.*

ON WRITING SCHEDULES AND BURSTS

LAURA FRASER: I try to approach writing like a regular job, where I work a seven or eight hour day. I go to an office outside my home. I schedule my writing time. If you wait for the muse to strike, you will be waiting for the rest of your life.

CAROLINE KRAUS: While I was writing *Borderlines*, which was my first experience writing a book under contract, I made the fateful decision to live entirely on my book advance. I wrote all day, every day, to excess. I do not recommend this. I recommend putting in reasonable writing hours to both preserve sanity and achieve better creative results, and I recommend maintaining employment at all times—for your family's sake, as well as your own.

MAXINE HONG KINGSTON: It's fun to play with a daily schedule. I'll establish one: write four hours a day, write two pages, write twenty lines of poetry—then have a revolution: take the day off on weekends, rest on Sunday, write ten lines per day, write ideas only, no email until 3 p.m. After *Tripmaster Monkey*, I made up my mind not to write for a year.

FRANK McCOURT: I like to do it every morning. It's like running. I used to run a lot. If you don't run every day, it's very hard to get back to it. Right now I'm traveling, promoting this children's book, but when I'm finished, it's back to the coffee, and the pen, and the desk.

STEPHEN ELLIOTT: Sometimes it seems like I stare at a computer screen five days a week and on one of those days I write 4,000 words.

ELIZABETH GILBERT: I write regularly, but in bursts, if that makes sense. I don't always have a writing project actively going. Sometimes months have passed where I'm not working on a book or major article, and so there would be no point to writing every day. I'll do other things—travel, read, think about my next book, shop, eat, whatever. But when I am working, I work the same diligent hours every day. Essentially I keep elementary school hours—at my desk by 7 a.m., a few breaks through the day, finished by 3 p.m. I don't have the stamina for some of the more wild habits of other writers—none of this "fugue state" business for me, and you'll never see me going two weeks without sleep while the words pour forth and I lose tracks of days. Like an elementary schoolkid, I need at least eight hours of sleep a day in order to function, and peanut-butter crackers help, as well.

Sometimes I wish my writing came to me in more dramatic bursts, but the good news is this—as somebody who's cultivated steadfast habits, I've never been burned dry by writer's block, either. Writing is my life and love, but it's also a job, and I was raised by a Swedish farmer: I know how to do jobs.

DAN KENNEDY: My schedule varies a lot. I have my own business, I travel a fair amount, I steal time to write wherever I can find it. Today I'm in New York at my writing space downtown, kind of locked in here because I know I'll get what you're reading here onto the page if I stay put. It happens to be a 3 p.m.-6 p.m. shift for writing today. Tomorrow I won't write, because I have other work to get done.

DAVID RAKOFF: I stay in pretty well all day, in the hopes that I will write. I try to keep lunches and such to a bare minimum. That seems important for me. That said, I probably only manage to write for ten minutes at a time before I have to distract myself with something.

JANICE ERLBAUM: I write five days a week, Monday through Friday, like a regular job, and I work in two-hour sessions. I do two hours of writing, then I take a lunch break, then I do another two hours of writing. Sometimes I quit after that, if I have something else to do— administrative work, or research, or meeting a friend—some days I get in another two hour block. But six hours is the most that I can work in a given day, and if I get four hours done, I'm happy. Even if those four hours weren't the most productive, at least I showed up and tried—I tell myself that tomorrow will be better.

ISHMAEL BEAH: I wrote six hours a day: three hours at night when all was quiet; one hour during the day to go over what I had written; and another two hours in the evening. I kept the schedule as best as I could but sometimes it didn't work. I always carried a pencil and a pad in my pocket so that I could write when things came to me outside of my scheduled writing sessions.

AZADEH MOAVENI: I usually get up extremely early, around 4 or 5 a.m., and write until late morning. I need the quiet of the early morning, and find I'm freshest at that hour. Then I take the rest of the day off, and go to bed very early. That's how I worked until I had a baby. Now I write in snatches, in the evening, whenever I can manage. Because I spend a lot of time thinking about what I'm going to write during the hours I spend with my baby, I do find that once I sit down behind the screen I have a better sense of where I'm headed.

PAUL COLLINS: I always write against a deadline, and I allocate a certain amount to write each day. Ideally, you want to leave a little note to yourself about what to start with the next day—just some sort of toehold to start that climb again.

AMY KROUSE ROSENTHAL: I am rather structured. When I'm in a "normal life groove," then my routine is to write daily from about 1:00–4:00 or 2:00–5:00. I do most of this writing out at coffeehouses. I do go through stages or phases of just having to wing it, to squeeze my writing in here and there when I'm especially busy or overextended with other stuff... by stuff, I mean, raising my kids, speaking engagements, speaking at schools, etc., and tending to other non-writing interests and commitments.

TANYA SHAFFER: I'm an afternoon writer. Back when I was making a chunk of my living as an actor and I had to go to the theatre every evening, I would spend most of the day procrastinating and get in a couple of hours of writing right before I had to leave. Now I'm a mom, and my time is more circumscribed. My son goes to preschool from 1:00 p.m.–5:30 p.m. and I basically get right down to it. Having such a major time constraint has made me much more efficient. I recommend it!

SARAH VOWELL: I'm oh so bursty.

ANTHONY SWOFFORD: Did someone say schedule? I liken myself to a long distance sprinter. I will work seven days a week for a month or six weeks and then take some time off to do research, to read, to annoy the people around me with childish pleas for attention and gifts. I try to get to work by 10 a.m., to write until 3 or 4, and then to return to the work for a few hours at night.

A.J. JACOBS: I try to write for several hours at a stretch. I find it takes me a couple of hours to get into the zone or groove, or whatever the kids call it nowadays. So the most efficient way is to do long unbroken stretches. Which is why I'm on a crusade to eliminate business lunches. I'm an advocate of the business breakfast. That way you can enjoy your waffle, then work for like eight hours straight. The lunch is just crazy inefficient.

FIROOZEH DUMAS: I'm a mom of three; I don't have a nanny or extended family nearby. This means I cannot stick to a regular writing schedule. My family always comes first so I write in spurts. I wrote *Funny in Farsi* on a 4:00–6:00 a.m. shift. With my current book, I write whenever I can steal some time. It's far from ideal but I still get done what I need to get done. I make the time. This means other things, like cleaning the house or seeing friends, sometimes fall by the wayside.

JULIA SCHEERES: I used to find I wrote best in the early morning (after getting my juices flowing by drinking coffee in bed while reading *The New Yorker*) but since I had my baby, I've been forced to change that routine. Now I don't get to my office until 10:30 or so, after dressing and feeding my daughter and dropping her off at daycare. Sometimes I use a goal-reward system. For example, after writing 400 or 600 words, I'll take a break and go down to the Marina for a cup of coffee, or fool around on eBay (a particular weakness of mine), or call up a friend to chat. My best advice is to use your most energetic time for writing if possible, and do the chores of life (cleaning, paying bills) in the downtime. Having a baby forces you to be very focused during the free time you have—you can't take your work home to do in the evening anymore. Be selfish with your writing time, reserving your best time of day for your manuscript.

STEVE ALMOND: I try to write in the mornings, because that's when I'm freshest, straight from self-propelled stories of dreamland. Also: I feel guilty if I don't write, so I'd rather get it done in the morning, so I can stop beating myself up by the afternoon. (Note: this rarely works.)

ON WORKING ALONE, OR WITH OTHERS

MAXINE HONG KINGSTON: I write with a community of war veterans once a season. I mostly work in solitude. I can write anywhere—on the beach, on airplanes and ships, in a corner of the living room with company around, in my studio alone. To get anything done at all, I feel that one needs to learn to create under all circumstances.

SARAH VOWELL: I write nonfiction and come out of a journalism background. The only community I've ever had or needed has been my editor or producer (to finish a piece or book, I mean). I think other writers are swell to hang out with at dinner, though.

JANICE ERLBAUM: I never would have started my book without a writers' group. I was terribly blocked for a few years—I knew I wanted to write about my life, but it wasn't coming—then I joined up with a group of friends, and we pledged to write and critique five pages a week together, no matter what. The first few batches of pages I wrote were awful, but they got better with practice, and I got into the habit of writing every week.

My first group fell apart when some of the members starting sleeping together, so I started a new group, and we've been meeting happily every other week or so for the past two and a half years. I'm incredibly grateful for their support, their commitment, their feedback, and the inspiration I get from them.

FIROOZEH DUMAS: I started out in a writers' group and it was really, really helpful. After about six months, I realized I needed to work alone. The group got me going and I have always appreciated them for that.

MATTHUE ROTH: I need to write alone. That said, having people to feed off of is incredibly important; and writing into a void will drive you crazy—imagine getting an idea, spending a year and 300 pages on it alone in your bedroom, and then showing it to your editor, going "Ta-da! This is my masterpiece about the breeding habits of mealworms." I have a group of three other local writers to meet with once a week. We swap ten pages of our stories, give each other criticism, and then we shoot the shit for an hour or two, just talking about our ideas and making sure they aren't about, well, mealworms.

STEPHEN ELLIOTT: It's easier on my heart in a community, but it doesn't make my writing any better. But it's nice to go to lunch with people. Writing can be very lonely.

ISHMAEL BEAH: I have only worked with one person. Never tried working with a community of writers. I prefer the loneliness, or writing with someone who understands that.

A.J. JACOBS: Just me, my old Mac, and my shade-grown Kenyan coffee. I would find other writers too distracting. It's like when I play my favorite nerdy game Boggle—I get all tense when other people are scribbling words down and I'm not.

ELIZABETH GILBERT: In my early twenties, I decided not to go to graduate school to get an MFA. I learned my craft, largely, through solitary work and my own discipline. But none of us are islands, and we all need feedback, too. So I started a writer's group (we called ourselves "The Fat Kids"—I can't remember why) and we met once every two weeks and shared our work with each other. In a way, I think this was better (and certainly cheaper) than going to graduate school. It was a wonderful resource. I wrote the entirety of my first novel under the tutelage and support of The Fat Kids. The main lesson that came of that arrangement was this—nobody can write your book for you, but the right voices can help encourage and motivate you when you've lost your confidence.

DAVID RAKOFF: I tried one of those writer's rooms for a while, but it made me need to pee and nap even more frequently than I already do—which is a whole lot—so I let my membership lapse. So now I stay home. I'm thinking of trying the reading room at the Yiddish Archive just down the street, though. It's pretty and quiet and has wireless. And surely I can't pee and nap more than a bunch of aging Yiddishists.

AMY KROUSE ROSENTHAL: By myself for sure. I love my writer friends, and we do have a great community here, but the actual writing, the pounding away, that I do solo. There are a couple people I run my ideas and drafts by, and that of course is awesome and helpful.

STEVE ALMOND: Well, I think you need a community of readers to keep you inspired, and offer constructive criticism of your work. But I'm always alone when I actually write. It's in a lonely place, I guess, where I need my characters, or ideas, or memories, as company.

OUTLINES vs. FREE-FORM

SARAH VOWELL: I used to be a real beatnik early on and my first book is a little too all over the place. Now, I depend on an outline. But I will say that I use outlines, in my books especially, as a way to bind together my all-over-the-place sense of narrative with a series of very fragile transitions.

FRANK McCOURT: As I went from page to page, one page would suggest the next, and I'd make notes as I went along. I know there are writers who are more deliberate, who have plans and outlines, but I didn't. If I had an idea I'd make a note for the next day. It's the way the people got in the Conestoga wagons to cross the country. You never know what you're going to find. You're dealing with your own life; it's back there, and it's a gold mine.

JULIA SCHEERES: I'm a journalist by trade, so I used an outline—it made me feel safer, thinking I had a roadmap to the book, or at least an itinerary I wanted to follow.

DAVID RAKOFF: I don't really use outlines and I both benefit and suffer for it. Actually, I can't see any benefit. I was going to say that no outline frees me up but that's just bullshit. I'd probably do better if I started with some sort of a framework. I'd still be able to free associate, but it might make it all seem less painful.

ANTHONY SWOFFORD: I generally sketched a few scenes ahead. I wrote the ending about halfway through the book. I wrote a page and I knew after I wrote it that it was the last page of the book, and then I wrote toward it. This was very beneficial, to have an end point tacked to the wall. But accidental. I couldn't have decided to do this, it had to emerge.

A.J. JACOBS: I'm a big fan of the outline. My books are written in bite-size chunks. Like 150 mini-chapters. I had to have some sort of blueprint, or it could just spin out of control.

PHILLIP LOPATE: I generally don't outline, but take notes, and then start to write, letting the process take me where it will. I don't know if that's "free form," but I like to be surprised.

JANICE ERLBAUM: I started the second draft of my first memoir by writing a book proposal, so I had to come up with an overview of the story and chapter summaries before the thing was even written. Basically, I wrote down everything that I thought should go into the book, put it in chronological order, and then tried to group the events into chapters. So I had a plan going into it, and I wound up being about 75 percent faithful to it in the final draft.

JONATHAN AMES: With novels, about halfway in, I will outline the rest of the story (as it usually comes to me around then), and then the outline might change, but it does become a roadmap. With essays, if I don't finish it one day, then I will often, at the end of the day, jot down what I see as the points I will have to hit to get to the end.

CAROLINE KRAUS: I did use outlines. I found making outlines restful and therapeutic. I still use the same system—a giant tablet of Rhodia graph paper that lets me see large amounts of information at once, on which I make diagrams, lists, storyboards, and timelines.

STEVE ALMOND: Well, I had a general idea of what I wanted to do. But I'd hardly call it an outline. I always *mean* to make an outline, I just never quite get my shit together enough to finish one. I must have, like, 5,000 unfinished outlines in my computer.

PAUL COLLINS: Because the travelogue and historical research in even my memoir work requires investing lots of time and travel, I can't write books on spec. So that means the book-pitching stage is crucial for me; I might spend a month apiece to come up with two or three book ideas, and then I sling them all at my editor and agent to see what they're interested in. Only then, when I have a contract, do I actually start. That book proposal process really forces me to outline very carefully what I'll be doing.

BETH LISICK: I decided on the thirteen stories I was going to write and wrote them in order of which ones I was most stoked about that day.

TANYA SHAFFER: I do a lot of outlining in all of my writing. I make outlines to help me keep the overall shape in mind. The outline isn't rigid, though; it's always changing. The key is to strike a balance between freedom and structure. I set up the structure to give myself a sense of direction, but I always allow myself the freedom to take off in unplanned and unexpected directions, much as I do when I'm traveling. Then I go back after the fact and adjust the outline to incorporate the new direction.

RACHEL HOWARD: Outline. Outlines are so reassuring. They give you the useful illusion that you know where you're going. And then I'd take little free-form excursions on the side.

MATTHUE ROTH: I'm a strict believer in free-form. That said, don't think there's a writer alive who doesn't outline in some way. You have to keep your thoughts organized in one way or another, and for me, that took the form of a (most of the time) two-page list of "things that need to happen"—an outline-like fact sheet, in order, that says things like "best friend dies" or "night I met Itta" or "cheesecake incident." They're all little memory-joggers, just to sort out the plot in my head.

AZADEH MOAVENI: Outline! I love outlining. I inevitably throw it out along the way, but the process is instructive.

Chapter VI

TRIMMING THE FACT

Killing your darlings when it's best for your book

Unless the reader is your mother or your stalker, chances are they will not find every aspect of your life enthralling. You can't include every bowl of cereal. You should probably mention the weekend in a Croatian jail, but maybe leave out the subsequent weekend doing laundry. In most cases, you will be hoping to write not the definitive account of every moment you lived, but a cross-section of that life that's readable, engaging and artful.

Writers tend to come in two models: packrat and Spartan. You probably know which you are already. If your teachers groaned under the weight of your thirty-page book reports, you're the former. Your challenge will be sorting out the filler from the material that moves the plot forward. If you do intend for people to read your story, editing — and making tough choices — is essential. If you want a scene showing your strained relationship with your brother, dig up a good memory that illustrates it best, one blow-out fight. You may end up conflating a few fights into one, in fact, and that's allowed. You fought a lot.

If, on the other hand, you had to set the margins to 1.5 inches and the font to 14-point to reach the book report page minimum, you're a Spartan. You'll need to bulk the text up. It's not padding: it's detail. Life is full. Many, many things happen, and if you're thirty years old and your memoir's only six pages long, you're not writing enough of them down.

But you'll get there. The more you immerse yourself in the manuscript, the more it will become obvious what needs to be fleshed out more and what needs to be cut altogether. Unfortunately, you may first have to write it all up and see how it hangs together. The good news is you can often recycle the fat later; the stories that just don't fit in this memoir can go in your next one.

CAPTURING WHAT'S INTERESTING AND CUTTING WHAT ISN'T

TOBIAS WOLFF: Memory is damn near infinite. Once you start unraveling that ball of string it just keeps coming. My method is to look for the patterns in the material. Things are not interesting just because they happened. There is a species of memoir that merely progresses from one event to another—"and then and then and then." The writer has not done the work of seeing what matters in all those "and thens." That's the greatest challenge in writing a memoir.

When you see certain patterns repeating themselves again and again, you don't need to repeat them constantly in the writing. You allow for things that are extraneous and incidental, but you're looking for the determinate patterns in your life. And that's the principle by which you finally organize your material.

FRANK MCCOURT: I do cut. Especially for *Teacher Man*. As much as was published, I discarded. I'm sorry I threw it all away. I was desperate, despairing. I should have kept it, there was probably some good stuff in there. But I have it in my head. If I want to write a novel, I'll use that.

The parts I cut didn't move the story forward and they didn't belong—digressions, things that happened to me or observations. I knew it was dishonest to put in those things, because—if you'll excuse the word—"artistically," or mechanically, it didn't work.

JAMES MCMANUS: I like to write very long, thick, messy drafts, then cut back, sculpt and hone.

LAURA FRASER: I cut about a third out of my final manuscript. Sometimes it helps to have an editor take a look, which I did—I paid a freelance novel editor to read it, and she had great suggestions. I chopped out whole chapters, mainly because they interfered with the pacing, or just focused too much on something other than the story, extraneous stuff about me. Remember, it's not about you, it's about the story. Anything in a memoir that's not in the service of the story should be cut. Nobody cares if you go to yoga on Tuesdays or eat yogurt for breakfast unless those details contribute to the story or to the character that is you.

JONATHAN AMES: I do a lot of cutting—if I'm reading my own piece and I get bored, it has to go. My goal is always to engage the reader, to never bore the reader, to entertain the reader.

ISHMAEL BEAH: I realized that I couldn't write about everything in my life, that there were many stories within my experiences and I needed to focus on one, which was a brief explanation of life before the war, life during the war and life after the war. Even with this decision, I knew I couldn't include everything, just what I felt important to make the point I had in mind. It is difficult making this decision but the reality is you can't write about everything in your life. You will never complete your work and at some point you will have to be satisfied with what you have written.

ELIZABETH GILBERT: You can only learn how to do this with experience. I had to figure out how to trim down my thousands of pages of notes (based on a year's worth of travel around the world, and two years' worth of serious contemplation and research) and turn that slush of words somehow into a book which somebody could actually digest.

Here's what helped: reading sections of my journals aloud and looking for the places where I was boring myself. This was my experience, my adventure, and if it wasn't interesting to me, it surely wouldn't interest anyone else. And reading aloud is always helpful because your ears are usually wiser than your eyes. Your eyes cheat, they skim across the page, they don't "hear" things that are wrong with your writing. Your ears are sharper, older, smarter, and less patient. Your ears will notice that you used the word "awesome" ten times in a paragraph, while your eyes might not notice.

DAN KENNEDY: I think after growing up on movies and TV I have this sensibility of, "What's the point of this scene? What does this chapter buy us in the story and time line?" On the book I'm writing now, I wound up in that situation where you have two beautiful chapters—two chapters that feel like some of your best writing—but they're both serving the exact same purpose in the overall story. So you have to cut one of them. I suppose you could also say that writing a book is all about indulging a story without the constraints of something super-commercial like TV or a screenplay, but I always feel like it's my responsibility to respect the reader's time and respect the fact that they've got a life and responsibilities, too—and they're taking the time to read your book—it feels like you have this responsibility to make the story as strong and engaging as possible. To make sure it's not dragging along just because you had these personal feelings that prevented you from making a cut.

PHILLIP LOPATE: Generally I over-write, then cut back. I write down everything I can think to say; then I read the results and try to shape the piece into an elegant form. Here, pace is the most important thing; if I feel I've been going on too long for the payoff, I cut.

DAVID RAKOFF: I don't know what to cut until it's all largely written. Writing is not like painting or cooking with salt. You can absolutely take stuff away without doing violence to the material. The more detail you can get down in the beginning, the greater your choice in deciding what to leave in and what to relegate to the file you keep of stuff you can use later, or not at all. Writing is about making choices.

Even the most minimalist language—especially the most minimalist language—requires that the things left standing are the Platonic ideals of themselves.

As for what to cut, I love that adage, "You must kill the darlings." If I'm cherishing a turn of phrase or observation or joke too much; if it's standing like a tall poppy on a lawn and I can't bring the rest of the material up to its standard, then I cut it. With great reluctance, but I cut it.

SEAN WILSEY: It was hard to cut. My book is long and I felt like it needed to be long. I wanted to leave room for different tones to ease their way into the book and coexist, and if I compressed things I worried I would lose that. I wanted this to be a big, adolescent, here-I-am kind of book.

That said, I cut a ton of stuff. The criteria was: 1) does it advance the story? and 2) does it move me in any way? I'm incapable of cutting something that makes me laugh.

JANICE ERLBAUM: First you just write down everything, then you start sorting through it. Something may make a great anecdote, but if it's not connected to any of the other parts of your story, you've got to leave it out. You know you have to cut something if there's no way to segue to or from it to the rest of the story—if you find yourself writing, "Another interesting thing that happened was ..." then you probably have to leave that interesting thing for another time.

AZADEH MOAVENI: I never know what to cut and I hate cutting. Especially if I've taken a long while crafting a paragraph or a few pages, I'm loathe to edit it out. It requires the scalpel of my editor to get me to cut material.

STEVE ALMOND: This is the $64,000 question. The whole key to writing well is getting rid of all the material that isn't A-list. And the only way you can do that is to develop a critical faculty—what Hemingway called a "bullshit detector." That comes, ironically, not so much from reading your own work (which you can't see clearly) as from reading the work of other beginning writers. You'll start to notice the mistakes they make, how much B material they allow into their work, and eventually (and largely unconsciously) you'll start to eliminate this deadwood in your work.

A.J. JACOBS: I do a tremendous amount of cutting, especially since the topics I've chosen were absurdly large—the encyclopedia and religion. So there was far too much to say. I use myself as a tester. If I'm rereading a section for the fourteenth time and I'm still interested, then that's a good sign. I'm also a fan of showing it to a bunch of friends. Test market the thing. I don't put too much weight on what any one person says, but if 90 percent of my friends say, "That section on Portuguese literature didn't need to be ten pages. Maybe eight or nine would suffice," then I'll chop it down.

SARAH VOWELL: So much cutting. One solid way to find out what to cut is to read aloud. The parts that bore you stick out pretty obviously.

PAUL COLLINS: I try to pick representative events so that I can avoid redundancy altogether. The mark of a bad historian and bad memoirist alike is that you feel like you're reading their notes, and not an actual narrative. This is even true when the writing, on a sentence by sentence basis, looks good. It's not actually about the quality of the writing, but about the effect of it. I'll cut perfectly well-written chapters and passages because they don't really add anything more to what I've said already.

ANTHONY SWOFFORD: Cut repetitive stuff. Cut things that don't propel narrative, that are self-indulgent (not that writing a memoir in the first place isn't self-indulgent, but you must forget that while writing). If you cut it and don't miss it, it probably didn't need to be there.

RACHEL HOWARD: I do huge amounts of cutting, or not so much cutting in the sense that I have a full manuscript and start hacking away, but trying out lots of material that I realize, far before the book is approaching full draft, doesn't belong there.

You have to remember that if you produce ten pages, and nine of them are useless, but one contains a memory you haven't considered in years, and suddenly it's seeming rich and significant—that's huge progress.

GUS LEE: Diane, my wife, has an uncanny ability to sniff out the distracting, self-indulgent detritus in my writing. I honor her cuts, even if they hurt, because I know she's right. My literary agents are also gifted editors. Thus, long before the manuscript lands on my publishing editor's desk, it's been repaired by three women of enormous professional talent. Then, my editor suggests further improvements before the merciless, hawk-eyed copy editor takes her turn. The only thing that gets wounded in this process is my stupid, grasping ego.

MATTHUE ROTH: In *Yom Kippur a Go-Go*, we ended up cutting something like eighty pages—a quarter of the book. But all is not lost, and happy endings can still be had: two chapters subsequently got published in anthologies. Another thing is, when you're writing, leave everything in; when you're cutting, take everything out. After I finished writing, I actually had two running drafts of the manuscript that I was editing—one super-short, super-tight one to show to the publishers, and one longer "director's-cut" version for my edification—and, so that when publishers asked me to write more someplace, I didn't have to—I already had it.

KEEP IT TO YOURSELF

DAVID RAKOFF: I'm not a huge fan of full and unbridled disclosure, at least not for myself in a non-therapeutic setting (and even then I think one should exercise good taste). I have some fairly hard and fast rules about what I will and will not write about. As a result, I don't know that I'd describe myself as a memoirist at all, despite the fact that I've written two first-person books.

In general, I try to maintain a distinct line between my life, with its viable experiences and connections, and my work. I find it lends a much-needed authenticity to both. I like being able to walk to the corner to do my laundry or buy some tin foil without wondering whether I can get 300 words out of it. I decided early on that I wouldn't write about my family, or about sex, for example. I don't in any way think less of other writers who do open their lives up in their work, I just can't do it with any sort of comfort. I find writing in general sufficiently difficult, and it's made it a good deal easier to at least not have that constant "am I selling so-and-so out?" nagging at me on top of everything else.

A.J. JACOBS: If it involves my wife's private parts, I have to get her permission.

LAURA FRASER: It's best not to get too clinical about sex. As my editor told me, "Leave something to the imagination." Another writer told me, "Never use the verb 'to enter' when you're writing about sex. You only enter an auditorium."

RACHEL HOWARD: I'm shameless. I'll share anything about myself. Always have been that way. I find it very freeing. I don't like to be afraid of what someone might learn about me. If I put it out in the world, I own it. The difficulty for me lies in remembering that not everyone is so comfortable with having their personal details divulged. I'm not very discreet.

ANTHONY SWOFFORD: I'm willing to share anything that will make the book better. This includes damaging admissions about my character at a particular point in my life.

AZADEH MOAVENI: Because I'm rather prim by nature, and because my immediate family (mother, husband, etc.) are rather conservative when it comes to anything sexual, I've drawn the line there. This actually came up recently when I was writing about the elective c-section craze in Iran, and I had to decide whether to mention that many women choose them to maintain their vaginal tone.

DAN KENNEDY: If we've dated—been in a relationship together— you don't have to worry about ever walking into a Barnes & Noble and reading about it. Beyond a kind and gentlemanly mention if we happened to be at a concert together or something, and you'll have seen it and had the chance to approve it way beforehand.

PHILLIP LOPATE: I have been told by my wife that I am not to write about her or our daughter. So far I've only violated her wishes a few times. We shall see. I am willing to share all parts of my own life, in principle, and the only consideration is how it will affect those others I write about, especially those closest to me.

MATTHUE ROTH: I do have boundaries, but when I'm writing, I try to ignore all of them—it interferes with telling the story. So go away, write your book, and then come back. Finished? Good. Anything you wouldn't say to your grandmother's bridge group, don't publish it. (Acceptable things to say can include a lot of dirt, sex, and sailor talk. Old people are saucy. Try it out.)

Chapter VII

MEMORIES MAY DIFFER

Writing respectfully, truthfully, and well about people who aren't you

In all likelihood, your memoir will include your friends and family. Because they are not getting an advance, some of them (perhaps understandably) might object to showing up in your book, especially in any scenes that involve things they'd rather forget. This is a tricky business, and it requires tact, diplomacy, and, sometimes, fearlessness. It also requires skill. How do you translate your loved ones—and less-loved ones—to the page? Do you mention their perms and gabardine slacks? The hash-mark wrinkles around their mouths from a lifetime of pursing their lips? And then there is the fear that you will depict them so accurately that they will call their lawyers. How do you weigh your right to tell your own story against someone else's right that you not *tell theirs? Then again, most authors find that their family and friends get upset not about being in your book, but about not being in it enough.*

THE GOLDEN RULE(S)

FIROOZEH DUMAS: I have a simple rule: If it involves me, I can write about it. If it involves others, I often get their permission. If it involves me *and* others, and I need to have them in my story, regardless of how they feel about it, I aim for fairness. In *Funny in Farsi*, I wrote about my mother-in-law with whom I had a horrible relationship. It was really challenging because a part of me really wanted to let her have it but I ended up only sharing what I had to in order to tell *my* story. We now get along really well and no, we have never discussed the book. Assuming she read the book, I like to think she realized that I was not trying to be mean but was just telling my story.

Not every story I write is flattering, but I try to be fair. My intention is never to hurt anyone with my words. I just tell my truth and sometimes, my subjects don't like the way they have been portrayed. Since I do make every effort to be fair, it does not bother me that someone might complain. That's just part of life when you write nonfiction. I would never, ever reveal someone's secret or write something intentionally embarrassing or hurtful. That's what journals are for.

CAROLINE KRAUS: Keeping to the truth is my chief policy, though that is not reason enough to write about someone. I think it's a case-by-case decision, but in my view, knowingly hurting someone in print, even with the truth, had better serve an unimpeachable purpose. On the other hand, writers cannot control how people will react, and it may happen that feelings are hurt in spite of honest and honorable intentions. So it's something to weigh carefully in every instance.

ANTHONY SWOFFORD: The only policy about writing about other people is to be honest. They cannot counter honesty. My younger sister has asked me to never write about her, so I won't. Everyone else is fair game.

TOBIAS WOLFF: With the exception of my immediate family, I always change the names of other people. I will often change their occupations. I do what I can to keep the essence of a person's character and behavior, but I try not to leave such a trail that he or she would be embarrassed by a friend reading the book.

JONATHAN AMES: Try not to hurt anyone. But this doesn't have to be the rule for all writers. You have to be fearless as a writer and as a consequence, people can get hurt. I have hurt some people—though I've only been confronted once—but it's something I really try to avoid.

DAVID RAKOFF: Avoid the ad hominem attack. I once interviewed a congressman at a party while he was eating. His table manners were bad. Terrible, in fact. Car accident-like. I can make myself skip meals even now just thinking about them. I think he managed to get crème caramel on his *glasses*. But I didn't use it because it had nothing to do with the story or what he believed. Save it for the fiction, I suppose.

ART SPIEGELMAN: I was totally oblivious when I was doing *Maus*. There are issues. Maybe that's how fiction gets born. You want to say what happened but if you do you'll be sitting around with lawyers for the next twelve years.

ISHMAEL BEAH: You definitely have to ask the people you decide to write about. Not everyone wants to go public with his or her stories. You have to ask them to allow you to write about them the way you view them, relate to them, not how they view themselves. Be honest with them about this to avoid future confrontations.

FRANK McCOURT: There were certain things I left out, on the advice of my editor. I didn't want to hurt anyone, and I certainly didn't want anyone suing me.

NICK FLYNN: I think in one's drafts one should be free to write out whatever small-heartedness and pettiness and anger one can access, and then slowly cook this raw emotion down. In general, I think it's a bad idea to view writing a memoir as a chance to grind an ax, so whenever I find myself doing that, I tend to keep it to myself. Ax-grinding is perhaps better suited for op-eds or talk radio.

STEPHEN ELLIOTT: My primary rule is that I don't identify people in a way that would hurt their lives or their jobs. They might know I'm writing about them, recognize themselves, but I usually change enough so that their co-workers won't recognize them.

STEVE ALMOND: The only real policy I have is to honor your experience. Any other course—for instance, writing to seek revenge, or to make yourself look good—amounts to exploitation. You're not dealing in truth at that point.

PHILLIP LOPATE: I consider each time what the traffic will bear, in each circumstance. If the person is dead, I am tempted to be more candid. I have no set rules or guidelines in this area. It depends partly on how important the story is, and how much or little I am burning to write it.

I pick and choose when to write about other people, how dangerous it would be for me to confide their secrets, and stay away from those elements that I deem too harmful to them. That said, I have often given offense—you can't please 'em all.

JANICE ERLBAUM: I did leave out some people and events from my memoir, in some cases because there wasn't enough room or time to discuss them fully, and in other cases because I wanted to spare people's feelings. The problem is, you'll never spare people's feelings when you write about them—some people were angry that they were left out! And I didn't cut out anything that was really vital to the story—if an event told you something important about me or another character, I left it in, despite the fact that it could upset someone else.

Sometimes the truth hurts, but as long as it's the truth, it's fair game. However, if you're holding a grudge against someone, it's probably best not to write about them yet, until you've got some clarity as to why they acted the way they did towards you; otherwise, your book will come off as biased, and you won't be a reliable, relatable narrator.

There's no point in humiliating someone just because you can. Readers won't like you for it, and you won't like yourself.

AZADEH MOAVENI: If I cared enough about a given person's reaction, I would be certain to check out with them in advance what sort of detail about themselves they were comfortable sharing publicly.

PAUL COLLINS: It sounds simplistic, but if I'm not prepared to live with the results of someone seeing it and not liking it, then I don't write it in the first place. And if I am, then I do write it. Because they *will* see it, sooner or later.

ELLEN FORNEY: So far, so good. Most of my autobiographical work has been upbeat, though *I Was Seven in '75* was all about the joys of growing up in a non-traditional family. I'm currently looking down the barrel of a more difficult autobiographical story, though, and I haven't resolved this question. I assume most autobiographical artists wrestle with this issue. Exposing your own self is one thing, but exposing your friends, families, and even enemies takes either callousness, great sensitivity, or a careful balance of both.

ESMERALDA SANTIAGO: My only policies in writing about other people is never to be mean, even if they were, and to resist the urge to get even with all the jerks and ignoramuses that have crossed my path.

A.J. JACOBS: A friend of mine who is an investigative reporter taught me a brilliant trick. If she's ever writing a negative article about someone, she makes sure to say right up front that he or she is good looking. Appeal to their vanity. So then when you slam them later in the article, they won't care as much.

I did that with my brother-in-law. He's this Harvard-educated blowhard (a loveable blowhard, in case he reads this). So when I introduced him in my first book, I started out with a physical description:

I said he's moderately good-looking, not balding, and kind of resembles John Cusack, which all happen to be true. When he read the book, he called me and said, "Well, I came off like a cock, but at least you said I was moderately good-looking."

HOW SAID PEOPLE REACT

STEPHEN ELLIOTT: People don't always react well to being in my books. My father in particular has a problem with the way the father character is portrayed in my autobiographical novels. Often he'll contact magazines that review my work to "set the record straight." It's poisoned our relationship, which was pretty heavily damaged to begin with. Another problem is that when I write about my childhood, the time I spent in group homes and sleeping on rooftops, it reads as an indictment of bad parenting, so my father has an interest in making it seem not so bad. He remembers the group homes I was in as nice places to grow up and I remember them differently.

SEAN WILSEY: I got some weird reactions from various people. My stepmother threatened to sue me. My mother was all over the map with it. The nicest thing she told me was, "Sean, it's such an accurate portrait of so many people that I know that I've had to conclude it must be an accurate portrait of me, too. And so I'm really going to have to take a look at the fact that I come across that way."

And then there are tertiary characters who, to a person, have been really nice about it. I did get an email from an ex-girlfriend who said, "I will forgive you for just referring to me as a pack-a-day smoker who laughed at your jokes in history class instead of your girlfriend who gave you lots of blow jobs, because I understand that in a memoir there is not room enough for everyone." Not a response I expected—and not how I remember things at all!

So people will be all over the place. And you have to be true to what you remember, because who knows what they'll say.

FRANK MCCOURT: Generally, my family, my brothers and so on, were all excited. In the town of Limerick, I was unpopular with some people. It was a very small group, and they got all the publicity. Squeaky wheel gets the grease, as they say in America.

ALISON SMITH: I was the first person in my family to go to college. When I came home in the middle of my freshman year and announced that I was going to be an English major, my father shook his head. "We work in factories," he said. "What are you going to do, work in an English factory?" Years later when I decided to try to write a book, he thought that was just about the worst idea I'd ever come up with, worse even than being an English major! So I was really nervous about showing him the book. Finally, the summer before publication, I got up the courage to send him a copy of the manuscript. He read the entire book in two days. He called me and said, "You're a good writer, baby. You did a good job!"

My mother died two months after the book was sold. She never got a chance to read it. But my mom was never accepting of what she called "my lifestyle." While she was dying, she had this code for how we would talk about things. If I went to a movie or I was reading a book and she asked about it, she would say, "Would I like it?" "Would I like it?" was code for: does it have any lesbian content? I had to say, Yes, if there was no lesbian content, and No, if there was lesbian content. I always followed her rule. In the one conversation I had with her about the book, she asked me, "Would I like it?" I decided to break her rule. I told her what I think is the truth. I said, "Mom, I think you'd love it."

RACHEL HOWARD: Most of them were fine with it. I knew the book would be very emotional for my grandparents (my father's parents) and wasn't sure if they'd read it. At some point I decided they must not have read it, and for a while that was disappointing to me, but I appreciated that they never spoke ill of it. I thought it was simply an intense subject for them and that was fine.

Then just last month I learned from my uncle that my grandparents have been deeply upset about the book for the last two years but never told me. I wish I had known because I could have talked to them about it. Now my grandmother has died. In fact, I was right—they never did read the book. My grandfather got to a line in the first chapter in which I describe him as having "dirty blonde hair" and took it as a slight. He decided I was trying to depict the family as a bunch of unhygienic rednecks. Obviously relations between us are such that anything I'd written would have upset him. I just wish he'd told me so that we could have had a conversation about it. Now that I know, I'm getting a clear signal from my uncles that it's not okay for me to talk to my grandfather about any of this.

My father's third wife Sherrie is depicted quite unflatteringly in the book, and this was a huge ethical quandary for me. I tried to be as fair to her as possible, but I decided that I had to be truthful about how I'd felt about her. Of course, it's extremely charged because members of my family have long suspected her of being involved in my father's death. I don't know if she has read the book, but I suspect she has.

I have no regrets about how I depicted anyone, except for one line in which I describe a college boyfriend as a "pimply-faced nice guy." The pimply-faced comment was simply uncalled for.

ELIZABETH GILBERT: [They reacted] very well, actually. But I was careful—very careful. Particularly when it came to writing about my ex-husband, I was terribly careful. I didn't use his name and I shared as few details as humanly possible about the reasons our marriage fell apart or the details of the divorce. If I could've written about divorce without writing about my divorce, I would have—but I had to mention at least some information. But I was very careful and, I hope, very respectful. For the most part, though, I haven't encountered big problems when it comes to writing about real people, mainly, I think, because I don't write from a place of malice, but usually from a place of love. I've heard it said that there are two kinds of writers—satirists and celebrants. I'm a celebrant. I don't want to write about people if I can't celebrate them, and so—even when I describe people's flaws—I think they know that, in my heart, and at the end of the day (or page), I am loving them and presenting them in the best possible light. If somebody is anything less than worth loving, they aren't likely to show up in my writing.

PHILLIP LOPATE: You can never anticipate how people will react to what you write about them. In my book *Being With Children*, I drew some portraits of teachers that were critical, and they did not bat an eyelash; other teachers, whom I did not write about, were offended. Sometimes you can write very favorably about someone in a paragraph or a page, and they resent being a cameo in your story when they see themselves as the center of the universe.

FIROOZEH DUMAS: Almost everyone loved it. One person told me not to include her in my next book. The relatives I left out were more upset.

ANTHONY SWOFFORD: In the end most people were happy to be in print. One guy thought he didn't get enough ink so he was a bit upset.

BETH LISICK: My parents reacted strongly at first, in a negative way. I portrayed them as the lovely angels they are, but what they were bummed about were the personal things I revealed about myself. I have a good relationship with them, and they thought they knew me pretty well, but the allusion to sexual relations with a butch dyke and the disclosure about the abortion were a little much to take. I felt really bad. I didn't want them to be ashamed of me. Luckily, twenty-four hours later they forgave me and threw a party for me at their house with a big deli tray from the supermarket.

LAURA FRASER: The main character loved it. He was incredibly flattered. My Italian friends liked it, too, although they don't read English, so they're not sure what I said. One guy I dated called to say that he didn't know that I didn't like him. This was after a date I wrote about where he told me that if I had plastic surgery on my nose, I'd be pretty. It was a funny story and revealing about my bad dates at the time, and I have to say I wrote about it without considering his feelings. I'd write it again.

JONATHAN AMES: I try never to hurt anyone or unduly expose anyone, and so for the most part no one has been hurt or offended. Then again not all people I've written about have read my books.

DAVID RAKOFF: I don't really write about people I know. I keep on waiting for one woman from one of the chapters to show up at a reading with a vial of acid, but she hasn't yet. For the most part, as I said before, I try really hard not to sell people out who might not necessarily have signed on to be written about. On the other hand, if you're a gay Republican advocating vile policies against your own best interests and supporting a false, immoral war so you can keep a tax cut? Then, sorry ...

JANICE ERLBAUM: Most of the people who appeared in my book felt that I'd portrayed them, and myself, honestly, so they were okay with the book—even some people who I'd portrayed as kind of jerky emailed me to say they understood why I'd written what I had, and forgave me for writing potentially hurtful things. But some people felt embarrassed by their actions in the past, and did not like to be reminded of them by what I'd written. They've been less than forgiving. The person who was angriest about my book was someone I left out—"Wasn't I important to you?" she asked. She was, but there wasn't room to write about everyone. So she felt my book was dishonest, because she wasn't included.

STEVE ALMOND: It's always a mixed bag. Some are thrilled for the attention. Others feel misrepresented, or exposed, and get upset. In the end, you have to be able to tell yourself that you tried your best to tell the truth about the people you wrote about. That's your essential job. The rest depends on how your subjects react, which is up to them.

It depends on the context. I'm sure old girlfriends don't necessarily appreciate showing up in an essay, but the guys who run the candy companies I wrote about in *Candyfreak* were pretty psyched to be written about.

GUS LEE: I think my West Point classmates who were largely identified had a hoot about appearing in the story; the tales I related were true and those times are always cause for either instant mirth or deep reflection. Ditto for my D.A. colleagues in the fourth novel, my Army buddies in the third, and my relatives in the fifth.

Everyone named in my nonfiction work on courage appeared by individual consent. My guess is that they, being humble and courageous leaders, were a little embarrassed by my extolling their strengths.

I haven't asked the villains in the true stories how they felt about appearing in print. One notable is serving multiple life terms and three had promising public careers truncated by the events I described. In some cases, I don't know what has happened to the antagonists who, at one time, had worried me and others, so much.

AZADEH MOAVENI: I found people's reactions utterly unpredictable and mysteriously subjective. People I imagined would be furious were grateful and understanding, and people I reference so fleetingly and benignly that I hadn't even anticipated their reaction ended up wanting to challenge me to a duel.

MATTHUE ROTH: Most people were okay with it—a surprising few were even excited. One person asked to be hugely disguised, which I did. I had to change parts of the story, for which I complained loudly and excruciatingly and, in the end, left to my editors—who removed one line, changed another, and actually solved all the problems.

DAN KENNEDY: There seemed to be this understanding that they would receive a substantial discount on the book, which really rubbed me the wrong way. We had a family meeting and I made it perfectly clear that they were to pay full retail. I think I eventually softened up a bit and offered them an educator's discount on orders of more than fifteen copies at a time.

ON SHARING DRAFTS
WITH PEOPLE IN THE BOOK

STEPHEN ELLIOTT: I show people drafts and things I've written about them. It really helps to show people stuff before they find it on their own. People are much more forgiving when you show them something in advance.

PAUL COLLINS: My wife sees my drafts, because she's always my first editor. But no, nobody else does. Honestly? It's because writing is how I make my living—so my drafts are quite literally nobody's business but my editor's.

ALISON SMITH: I did not show drafts to the people portrayed in the book till after it was sold and scheduled for publication. At that point I sent it to the "characters" represented in the book along with a letter expressing how much it meant to me to be able to include them in the book and telling them that I ardently hoped that they would find their portraits loving and accurate. I did not offer an opportunity for the people portrayed in the book to suggest changes. I think that's a slippery slope. You can only please one master and that is the writing. So unless the situation really calls for it, I would not go looking for editorial feedback from the people represented in your book.

RACHEL HOWARD: I showed my mother a full first draft. The thing about my mother is that she was a very good mother but she remained married to an asshole second husband for ten years even though she knew that second husband hated me and screamed at me. I also revealed in the book that my mother once had an abortion, in order to leave that marriage.

My mom had no problem with me writing about the abortion. She read the full draft and came to me and said, "You're making too many excuses for me. You're trying to explain away my marriage to Howdy. You're going to have to be harder on me if you want it to be a good story."

I thought that was incredibly brave and generous of her. And she was right. I cut all the excuse-making and let the story stand on its own.

BETH LISICK: I did ask my mother-in-law if it was okay if I revealed that she went to a fisting demonstration at the Sex Workers' Art Show and she gave me the thumbs up. I just wrote something for my new book about being a guest in a well-known person's house. He didn't know I was going to write about it, so I sent him the section for his approval. Do unto others and all.

FIROOZEH DUMAS: Oddly enough, my two oldest kids are my best editors. They read every story and have lots of comments. I often make changes based on what they say. I also have one friend who gives great feedback but she's quite a busy person so I don't use her that often. When she does make a comment, I listen. I don't have anyone read drafts unless I respect their judgment. Otherwise, their comments just annoy me.

DAN KENNEDY: I didn't show anyone drafts of *Loser Goes First*. And that's something I've changed. I show friends a chapter now if they're in it. I ask them if they'd like their name changed or left as their real name, because in a weird way coming up with fake names for friends just seems so precious and self-important to me. It seems, just very, "Ooooh, look at me, I'm a writer! I'm changing your name!"

Although it should be noted that this time when I asked my friends Ben and Nat if they wanted their names changed, they took it as an opportunity to haze me. Me: "Do you guys care if I use your names in the new book, or would you rather I change them?" Nat says, "Call me Bryce. Or I'll sue you. As a matter of fact, start calling me Bryce even when you're not writing about me. You're the only friend I want to call me Bryce." Ben said he would take legal action against me and my publisher unless his name was changed to "Suck It." My own girlfriend said she wanted her name to be Krystal Cheri. Ha ha, very funny. Why do I even hang out with these people?

STEVE ALMOND: I showed drafts of *Candyfreak* to lots of my friends, all throughout the process. They were gracious enough to tell me how sucky many parts were, in a manner that allowed me to make them less sucky.

LAURA FRASER: I showed the main character a draft. He did not ask for any changes, except that I leave out some details about his family, which I agreed to do. The story was about him, and to mention them was an invasion of their privacy.

ELIZABETH GILBERT: I showed everyone who's in the book a copy before we went to print, in order to make sure people were comfortable with how I'd depicted them. But I am not in contact with my ex-husband anymore, so I knew I wouldn't have that chance—another reason to be very, very careful and restrained in writing about him.

JANICE ERLBAUM: I didn't show anybody drafts. I don't think I will for the second book, either. If someone wanted me to change what I wrote, they would have to have a really good reason, like if I'd been factually mistaken about something and not known it.

PHILLIP LOPATE: I show no one my drafts of autobiographical works about them beforehand. Why give them the power?

MATTHUE ROTH: I never show anyone anything until I'm absolutely finished writing it. I don't want people to see the story when I'm midway through. I especially don't want to start worrying about what people will think, because then I'll be writing either angels or eunuchs.

ON DEPICTING
REAL PEOPLE ACCURATELY

DAN KENNEDY: Accurately? When most of the egg is on your face, you are rarely challenged on your arguably insensitive depiction of loved ones. That's something I learned early on. Plus, it's actually quite accurate that I've described my aunt as an emasculating wannabe Marxist who doesn't let a layman's limited understanding of nutrition keep her from openly judging the eating habits and body shapes of others. That right there is just plain, old-fashioned, good reporting. When I know I've hit it right on the money like that, Aunt Pat isn't going to see a draft before it hits bookstores nationwide. What does she need to approve? The truth? That would be just like her, wouldn't it?

SEAN WILSEY: I've been reading *History of My Life*, by Giacomo Casanova, and the guy really knows how to draw a character. He can make you see someone in a paragraph. But mostly he just makes you see *him*. That's what comes through with Casanova: you're seeing the other people *through him*. And there's something very revealing about that. So the way he describes *them* adds to how you understand *him*. Reading Casanova is a good place to start if you want to get an idea of how to do it yourself, *and* the mistakes you might avoid. Also, talk about inability to cut ...

A.J. JACOBS: I think conversation is crucial. The way people talk reveals a huge amount. Also, I strive for the telling detail. I don't always nail it, but I strive for it. One detail is worth a thousand words, to co-opt a cliché. Like with my pretentious brother-in-law, I pointed out that he uses a Latin aphorism in his email sign off. That sums him up.

For *The Year of Living Biblically*, I attended a meeting of the New York Atheist club. It was at a Greek restaurant. And there were thirty people there, and they asked for thirty separate checks. I thought that was a good insight into radical atheism.

STEVE ALMOND: Most people are actually pretty good observers of other people. We all spend a lot of our lives making judgments about the people we meet, running smack or singing praises. The most important thing when you're writing about other people is simply to pay attention. To notice the things that make someone who they are—again, all that stuff we often take for granted: how someone walks across a room, or the expression on their face when they're talking about something painful. It takes a lot of effort, and humility, to put aside your own thoughts and really perceive someone else. But it's the only thing that allows you to empathize with them in the way that produces a true portrait.

PAUL COLLINS: I don't include physiognomy, because I find it irritating. I don't care about someone's cheekbones, so I won't allow my reader to either. Dialogue is generally how my characters emerge. You reconstruct dialogue that is recognizable to you and your subject as something you both think was said. Just because you distinctly remember someone saying something doesn't make it useable: if it's out of context or out of character for them, then it becomes your word versus theirs. And you, writer who didn't take notes at the time, will lose that fight.

BETH LISICK: I love describing clothing and watching the way people move. It can tell you so much about someone if you can get at how they carry themselves. And body parts and shapes! I love to describe hands and butts!

TANYA SHAFFER: The rhythm of speech and the words a person uses are particularly important to me in capturing that individual's unique character. Beyond that, I try to make others notice whatever it was that

I noticed about each person. I ask myself what I noticed first and try to recreate that moment. Was it something visual: unusual height, weight, eye color, style of dress? What did I notice about the person's voice when he/she spoke? Was it fast or slow, high-pitched or low, gravelly, hard to hear so that I had to lean in? I ask myself too what I remember most vividly about the person's character and way of being. Did he or she live passionately or lackadaisically? Any unusual habits, opinions, enthusiasms? My goal is to create a complete experience of an individual's uniqueness by recreating the details that stand out most sharply in my memory.

JANICE ERLBAUM: Well, I always change little things like hair color, or someone's job, but I try to keep the essence of their personality as true to life as possible. Their speech, their word choices, their inflections, their mannerisms, the way they dress, their ethnic identity, and, most of all, their actions should be true to life.

LAURA FRASER: It's important to really listen and take notes on conversations—the patterns of speech people use, the phrases. I always describe people's clothing, because clothing tells a lot about not only how stylish someone is, but also about how they spend their money, whether they are fairly conservative, whether they have a little quirk. The professor in my book always wore a scarf; a long, worn jean jacket; and a heavy silver bracelet, which pins him as a certain kind of Frenchman. He also has a distinctive nose, and watery blue eyes, so I mentioned those, as well as his curls. As he told me, "You described me so well that people who don't know me are going to come up to me on the street and ask about the book." In one case, in Paris, that actually happened to him.

DAVID RAKOFF: I include whichever details jump out at me and seem eloquent. Sometimes it's the way they look, other times it's their word choice, or the timbre of the voice. It will be different for everyone, so stay alert.

PHILLIP LOPATE: I try to be just—that is, not to write out of revenge or malice, but to put myself in their shoes as much as I can. Beyond that, I use the standard techniques of literary portraiture: physical description, habits, emphasis on idiosyncrasy and contradiction.

MATTHUE ROTH: In order to make real people into characters, change some physical details about them. It's the easiest way to make them into new people, forcing you to breathe life into them on their own—you can't just rely on the crutch of your friendship (or enemy-ship, or casual sex-ship, or whatever) to make them into interesting people on a page. Change their eye color from brown to hazel, or from hazel to purple. Make them really tall or really short. Give someone a hunchback.

To that end, I change everyone's name from the beginning—that way, I'm thinking of them as both a person and a character in a book.

ON WRITING ABOUT FAMILY

STEVE ALMOND: Yeah, that's a big issue. My family is pretty good about this stuff. But a lot of people have trouble with being written about. They feel it's embarrassing, or best left private. There's no way around this. You have to believe in the mission of what you're writing about, and not censor yourself. You can't write scared. At the same time, if you think a family member is going to be devastated by what you write, you need to think about what's more important—your memoir, or that person's feelings.

STEPHEN ELLIOTT: They reacted terribly. My father used to joke, "I only handcuffed you to a pipe one time and look how many stories you've written about it."

FIROOZEH DUMAS: The people who were the most upset were those relatives that I did not include in my stories. They assumed I did not love them enough. Oy.

PAUL COLLINS: Mine was an unusual case, because I was writing about a non-verbal child—first because he was a baby, and then because he's autistic. Morgan's autism is quite apparent when you meet him—it's not as if this is a secret, and so why treat it that way? And so I wrote very forthrightly about him. He is who he is and there's nothing to apologize for or be ashamed of in that. But I would be ambivalent in writing about a typical child—someone who might be very self-conscious about what I said.

A.J. JACOBS: They were okay with it. *The Year of Living Biblically* was a little tense—I wrote a lot about the black sheep of the family, this guy who used to be married to my aunt. He's a bizarre character —he used to lead a cult, he's now an Orthodox Jew in Jerusalem. My family doesn't like him. But he was just too enticing a character to leave out. So I went ahead and met him without telling my family. And then I showed them the chapters after I'd written them. They weren't happy, but it was a fair portrait of him, a warts-and-all characterization, so they ended up forgiving me.

ESMERALDA SANTIAGO: My family has been very generous about the way they are portrayed in my books. They understand that this is my version of events, the way I experienced my life, even if they were a part of it.

DAN KENNEDY: In all honesty, they were really cool. That's a pretty bland answer, I guess, but it's the truth. Early on my dad said, "Anything with us is fair game if you can get some material out of it."

JONATHAN AMES: When my first novel came out, my parents and I went to a family counselor and I was able to tell my parents what was true in the book and what was not true. Since then, they've become increasingly accepting, if not inured, to what I write.

AZADEH MOAVENI: Some of my relatives were astonishingly petty, upset that I hadn't depicted their class status properly. I have a branch of the family that is still not speaking to me, though I suppose I'm better off than other Iranian memoirists I know, who've been threatened with lawsuits by their relatives.

JULIA SCHEERES: I no longer have a relationship with my parents as the result of my memoir. But things were always strained between us, and I was okay with this possibility. In fact I found it tremendously liberating to write them and tell them I was tired of pretending everything was fine when it wasn't. We've never liked each other. There's always been a great deal of tension between us, for reasons explored in my book.

I guess some families are just like that—just because you're born into a family or to a set of parents doesn't meant you get along with them. My one goal in *Jesus Land* was to immortalize my brother David, to record his life. My allegiance was to him, not to my parents, who were physically and emotionally abusive toward him. I told them I wanted to drop the facade.

The most common question I get from readers is asking what my parents' reaction was to my book. I know from the grapevine they have refused to read it, and have called it a "pack of lies" outright. That's fine, I don't seek their approval. The best feedback I get from readers is that they feel they know David after reading my memoir to the point where they sincerely mourn his loss, so I feel like I did my job.

GUS LEE: My father, even though I cleverly changed his name, somehow identified himself and absolutely hated being in print. Few families enjoy having their uncomfortable pasts revealed, and Chinese Confucian/Buddhist/patriarchal clans are no exception. Sadly, my sisters were unhappy that I had not only given our father a pseudonym; I had disguised him by omitting his many family crimes. They thought a former prosecutor ought to have done a better job. They were probably right. By the time I wrote the memoir *Chasing Hepburn*, I had found the ability to forgive our father. I admired his telling me the truth about his life. It was, and remains, a priceless gift.

SOME WORDS OF WARNING AND ADVICE

NICK HORNBY: I really didn't think anyone was going to read my book. I thought it would come out, maybe get a couple of nice reviews and die a peaceful death. But it sold a million copies in the U.K. and got translated into a lot of languages.

So when you're writing your memoir, imagine this: your next door neighbors will read it. Your dad's boss will read it. Your mother's book group will read it. You still think that joke about your sister's acne is worth it? Because she's going to get teased about it once a week for the next ten years. If this memoir is for your benefit, fine. But if you want it to be read, think hard about what you actually need to expose. I thought hard about the big stuff, not hard enough about the little stuff. And yes, I made a silly crack about my sister that both she and I regret.

TOBIAS WOLFF: You have to accept that other people are probably not going to like it. Nobody wants to surrender control of their story to someone else. Generally speaking, I've fared pretty well with my family. My father was dead. My stepfather certainly hated my first memoir, but my mother took it in stride. She thought it was 80 percent true, which is actually a pretty good score.

If you allow the concerns of family members to impede the writing of what you consider your story to be, you'll never write. You'll be held hostage to their anxieties. But I sympathize with those anxieties. "They can write their own damn story" is not an answer—not everyone can write, and it doesn't really let them reclaim their privacy. There's always going to be a sense that you've transgressed on the privacy of others.

But like dictatorships and corrupt institutions, families have always been extremely secretive—they don't like to have anything but the authorized version of themselves presented to the public. But I think it's our privilege to write truthfully about the institutions that control our lives, and to tell our personal stories as well, even if those fly in the face of family mythologies that others have taken great care to nurture.

SEAN WILSEY: Make sure you know where you stand with your family. If you're going to burn your bridges, be sure you really don't love or need the people on the other side of them. I went into this knowing that my stepmother was pure poison and not caring if I ever spoke to her again. My mom was profoundly different. I wanted to tell the truth but I also wanted to continue to have a relationship with my mom, and that was really tricky. So know where you stand.

SARAH VOWELL: The only person who has had a problem with what I've written about myself is me. I wrote my most personal pieces for a fledgling public radio show, starting when I was twenty-six years old. I felt like I was revealing things about myself to the microphone in a studio in Chicago. Boy, was I surprised to find out there were people on the other end listening. Eleven years later, I'm way more reserved and careful about what I reveal. That probably makes me a less brave writer but I don't really care. I'm more cautious but I'm also more experienced, so I think that balances things out. Like, my earlier writing was more open and raw and immediate but I think it was also less profound and funny. I don't mind trading a little bravery for a dash of depth.

STEVE ALMOND: Well, you have to be willing to write about your subjects fearlessly, or you shouldn't write about them at all. If you're going to hold back on your family—or a particular experience, or relative, or dynamic—then write about other things first, ones where you can be rock-bottom honest. It's also true that you have to be able to go home again, so if there are relatives whose feelings you would hurt by writing about them, then you have to weigh that—not hurting them—against your desire to tell that particular set of truths to the world.

ALISON SMITH: You cannot think about how people will react to your writing while you are writing. Especially when you are writing a first draft. First drafts are for you. When you write your first draft I think you should close the door of the world and write the truest, most complete account you can. When you start to panic, thinking that you are revealing too much, or telling family secrets, or casting someone in an unflattering light, remind yourself that this draft is only for your eyes. Later, once you understand your material, you can choose what to reveal and what to conceal.

DAVID MATTHEWS: To anyone who doesn't like the way you've rendered them, tell them to write their own book. As a memoirist, your first duty is to tell your own story, as truthfully as you can. (This doesn't mean objectively—it means the emotional truths of an experience as it felt to you.) If you decide to write about family, your first concern should be the story, your concerns about family should be, like, fifth on your list. You're a writer, or you're not. You tell your truths or you don't. If you don't, you can still be a writer, but you won't be a very good one. My advice is make sure you don't get sued, but beyond that, write about anything and anyone that makes your story interesting. No matter what. If you wanted to be loved by everyone, you wouldn't be a writer, you'd be a camp counselor.

DAN KENNEDY: Just remember that there's a kind of dangerous dynamic with writing—you write alone, in some little secret room where you're enveloped in your own little reality, but the truth is, everything you're typing is going out of that place and into the world, so just remember that. You can get to thinking that you're typing to yourself in your little room, but you're really sending something out across the country. To people you haven't even met. I think if you keep that in mind, it's little harder to get in trouble.

AZADEH MOAVENI: Beware of the mischievous, invisible hand of your own subconscious!

FIROOZEH DUMAS: I hate it when people write memoirs to get back at their families. Go to therapy, keep a journal, work on your own stuff. Writing is not vengeance. A great example of this is Tobias Wolff, who writes about his stepdad. The guy was as awful as they get but the memoir is so much more than that. I could tell that by the time Tobias wrote his story, he had moved beyond the pain and was writing from the other side. For me, that is what makes the story compelling, and not the fact that the stepdad was awful.

ESMERALDA SANTIAGO: My only words of advice are that you should be ready to defend every word you publish in a book. So, don't lie, don't make up stories, and write about people in all their complexity. People are never all good or all bad. Look at the flaws as well as the virtues and you will write about real people, not caricatures. When people recognize themselves as complex individuals, they will be less likely to be rankled by their portrayal.

GUS LEE: I recommend letting your relatives and to-be-named or alluded-to friends know what you're doing. I would ask for their input and see if you can accommodate their wishes without impairing the integrity of your story, i.e., its fundamental moral imperative truths.

PAUL COLLINS: You'll live with your family a lot longer than you live with critics or readers. Measure your words accordingly.

Chapter VIII

YOU CONTAIN MULTITUDES

How your story is unique; how your story is universal

It's a memoir, and while you'll be writing about other people, you're primarily writing about yourself—in a way that perfect strangers will want to read. Memoir is a tricky business of making the personal universal.

It can take a few tries to get this right. Memoir is a one-man band: you're the subject, narrator, author, and editor; bassist, drummer, guitarist, and lead vocals. You don't have much narrative distance, and it can be hard to figure out how personal is too personal. Maybe your first draft is too detached. Maybe your second is one big overshare. It may be helpful to think of it as a novel with a protagonist who shares your name and life history. Many memoirists do.

You'll also have to decide how much of that history you want to reveal. You're the gatekeeper to your secrets, crimes, desires, and fears, and you alone decide what you're willing to share. Yes, it's art, but it's also life, and you'll have to live with the consequences. What are you willing to have your parents, your boss, your partner, and your mail carrier know about you? There's some value on erring on the side of discretion.

No matter what your approach, it's guaranteed that you'll be sick of yourself when you finish with this. But for now, you're the most fascinating thing in the world. Like Walt Whitman, you contain multitudes.

ON MAKING THE STORY
BIGGER THAN YOURSELF

DAVID RAKOFF: Sometimes it isn't. And then it goes into a drawer never to come out again. I suppose the thing to remember is that you are simultaneously unique and generic. You are the owner of the experience and have a viewpoint worth expressing (the secret bully that is the writer, to reference Ms. Didion), but you also understand that you aren't that special. The realizations and insights that you come to *have* to be felt by others.

The trick then is to not express them in a stupid or stultifying way ("And then I realized that when people ask 'How are you?' they sometimes *don't care about the answer!*"). If the insight gained is too specific and couldn't possibly be shared by the world at large—personal messages sent to you through toasters, sudden identification with dead members of the Hapsburg clan, a desire to rub cheese and feces into your clothing—then you might actually want to get that checked out.

LAURA FRASER: One important thing is to think of yourself as a character. I didn't think so much about *my* story as I did about the story of a thirty-six-year-old American woman whose husband leaves her and she makes a kind of mad dash to feel better, discovering some things about herself in the process. You have to ask the big questions: how do you get over heartbreak, what is it that makes us feel desired, what does travel do to our sense of ourselves, how do sensual pleasures transform us?

I think it's always best to step away and think of yourself as a character you would create in a novel, and ask what are the stakes, what are her flaws, what is her transformation?

SARAH VOWELL: Whatever personal story or anecdote you're recounting, try and figure out what it's about. For example, I once wrote an essay about my fascination with mafia movies and talked about how, when I was in college, I would watch part of *The Godfather* every day. That's an interesting predicament. But it was only in writing about it that I figured out that I was so lost at the time, reeling from losing my religion, pulled in so many directions by all the stuff I was reading about in my classes, that I needed to retreat into that movie's title character's stifling worldview. I was suffering from too much freedom, basically.

Then, the next half of the piece went to Sicily, where I had gone because of my obsession with that movie. And while I was there I ended up in this restaurant run by a close, closed family much like the one in the movie, which ended my preoccupation with the Corleones. Essentially, I realized that flailing around with too much freedom is the way of living that suits me. So the whole piece became a meditation on the problem and joy of freedom.

ELIZABETH GILBERT: I try at times not to write merely about myself, but about my Self—if that makes sense. Nothing is more universal than the Self—the capital-S human soul. The fears and doubts and ecstasies of the human encounter. Also, even though this was a memoir, it wasn't just about me; it was also about Italy, about India, about Indonesia, about God and about all the people I met along the way, whose stories I told in conjunction with mine. I wanted my readers to fall in love with the people I'd met along the way, as much as I myself had. While I technically traveled "alone," I was far from alone most of the time—and the wonderful souls and teachers I encountered kept me company and hopefully kept the reader company, as well.

DAVID MATTHEWS: Take what you think is your own personal story—"child of divorced parents falls in love with his new teenage stepsister," etc.—and step away from the specifics. What we have in that specific story is a universal story of forbidden love. Always look to see what your story has in common with other people's experiences. Everyone struggles with the need for love, acceptance, the search for identity; the overcoming of adversity—sometimes all of the above! Your story probably fits into one of these themes, and when you find it, start shaping the events of the story around that larger idea.

PAUL COLLINS: I try to make the story *literally* bigger than myself by including other people in it—by interviewing or reconstructing dialogue, by giving it a setting, and by seeking out the narrative arc intrinsic in it. The irony of memoir is that the best ones focus on people other than the author.

FRANK MCCOURT: All you have to do is tell the truth. It's as simple as that. We share common experiences. There are poor people all over the world, there are people who are troubled with relationships or religion or school. You just tell your story.

BETH LISICK: I think if you are writing about your family and your relationships, fears and humiliations, the universality is built in.

GUS LEE: Well, my stories are always naturally larger than me. But to emphasize the delta between the story and the writer, I try to use humor (my kids would say, *Nice try, Dad*) while constantly relying on larger, true-life characters. I'm lucky in every respect, especially with those with whom I've lived.

STEVE ALMOND: We all walk around in a constant state of desire and shame and sorrow and hope. So if I'm able to record those things in my life, other people will connect.

ESMERALDA SANTIAGO: I try to tell the truth as I remember it, to be as specific as memory allows, and to exorcise shame, which I think is one of the most self-destructive emotions a human being can feel.

PHILLIP LOPATE: I try to select just those experiences or observations to write about that I sense will "carry" or "tell" for others. The main way

I do it is to cultivate detachment and self-awareness, so that I am not being too defensive but am serving the piece of writing.

JANICE ERLBAUM: If you make sure to write about your *feelings* as much as you write about the events of your life, then readers will be able to relate to your story, even if they haven't experienced similar events. Everyone can relate to feelings of disappointment, shock, jubilation, betrayal, or what have you.

AZADEH MOAVENI: I think I had this technique of interrogating all of my content—all of my anecdotes, stories, experiences—and making sure it stood the test of "would this still be interesting to me if it had happened to someone else?" It's tricky, this business of being in the story, but not having the story be just about you. To an extent, though, I also learned the hard way. I had an editor who very gently would remind me to stop navel-gazing, and I would feel mortified for a moment, and then vow to be very careful in the future. No one wants to be a navel-gazer, and being super-conscious of how unattractive that is, I think, helps you focus on the rights part of your life, the universal parts.

TANYA SHAFFER: It's all about getting at the truth. I don't think we have to work to make things universal. We humans are more alike than we are different. Paradoxically, if we tell our individual stories with enough vivid particularity to bring them alive, they will be universal and people will connect to them.

RACHEL HOWARD: Stay in scene as much as possible. Let the reader experience the story with you.

ANTHONY SWOFFORD: The particular, finely rendered and emotive, becomes the universal. The abolition of the ego is also important. No, essential.

A.J. JACOBS: For me, the key is the subject matter. I like to combine my own life with something that's going on in society—whether that's information overload in *The Know-It-All*, or religion in *The Year of Living Biblically*. I try to alternate chapters, one on myself, one that's more reportorial about the topic. So in the Bible book, I'd have a chapter on disciplining my kid according to the Bible, then follow that with a reported chapter on my visit to the Amish.

FIROOZEH DUMAS: My theory is simple. Write your truth and people will relate. Truth resonates.

DAN KENNEDY: Stand on bridges that men died building, read the local news on any given day, and if you still think it's all about you, consider the fact that in the time it takes to read this answer people have been born someplace, people have died someplace, somebody's heart was broken, another person just fell in love, somebody else got some news they never thought they'd get—and all of this, by the way, is probably happening within a three mile radius of where you're sitting.

One day I was walking up Park Avenue pondering all of the most self-centered stuff; hmmm, is my life going the way I really want it to; do I really want to live in New York or should I move to California; I wonder if I really want to have kids—all of this me, me, me, bullshit—and all of a sudden a cab ran the light, came through the cross walk, up onto the sidewalk, and plowed into about six or seven people about fifty feet behind me. It was chaos to put it incredibly mildly. I'm on the phone to 911. Before I can even dial three digits, cops are running in from all sides, next thing you know, five or six ambulances—the medics are all running into the scene carrying white sheets, and it occurs to you that ain't exactly a good prognosis—the good news is, they didn't need to use even one of those white sheets. Everyone lived, but it wasn't all good news, I can guarantee you. There were six lives that changed massively in the blink of an eye. You witnessed that moment where lives change forever in ways that everyone hopes to god their life never changes. And, of course, that's a so-called small scale disaster compared to what I've seen in my time living here.

Now, by all means, let's write our books about our stories—it's valid, it's important, it's entertaining, it's what we're able to do—all I'm saying is there's a lot happening everyday in the blink of an eye, there's a lot of people living a lot of lives—we're not alone when it comes to living a life, and life is bigger than all of us.

HOW TO INCORPORATE
LARGER HISTORICAL EVENTS

ANTHONY SWOFFORD: If it's a personal memoir the practical scope of the book will be very small, the world that one person inhabited in the midst of these major events. It's important to focus on your small private world and to remember you are not writing a history of the event, you're writing *your* history of the event.

SARAH VOWELL: Be specific. In one of my books I write about that day in Kabul when the Taliban were ousted and people could play music for the first time in years. That was just one of the dumbest edicts ever—no music! I imagined giving up something as simple and as inalienable as chopping garlic in time to "Rock Lobster." My point being, something so small and seemingly mundane as cooking dinner while listening to the not particularly upstanding B-52s was a clean shortcut to pointing out the glaring idiocy of a political regime.

...AND TRANSLATING
CULTURE TO THE PAGE

AZADEH MOAVENI: By being self-deprecating and including the results of all my own knowledge gaps, all my own foibles and embarrassments. That way you're keeping company with the reader, and not so much in the didactic role.

FIROOZEH DUMAS: Ever since I was seven, I have basically been an unpaid ambassador. To some degree, this happens to all immigrants but I really took it to heart. I always wanted to make Americans understand Iran and vice versa. I can't seem to stop.

ESMERALDA SANTIAGO: I assume my reader is intelligent, and if I put things in context, she or he will understand. If it is still unclear, I believe my readers are smart enough to look things up.

GUS LEE: I wish I could claim a special gift, but being multicultural was involuntary, and it really helps.

But then, didn't *everyone* come from a Shanghai immigrant family, grow up in an inner city African American 'hood with a Pennsylvania Dutch stepmother, attend a Cantonese Catholic Chinatown school, learn street Spanglish, participate in a black church, and get raised by a polyglot Jewish/Italian/Filipino/Chinese/German/Mexican YMCA boxing faculty?

A different culture is scary when viewed through narrowed eyes and with a racing pulse; that same culture, viewed with a brave friend and an open heart, it becomes the world.

Chapter IX

GETTING THE JOKE

Reconciling Humorist with Memoirist

If you're lucky, you already have some laugh-out-loud material to work with. You just need to figure out which ones translate to the page. It's usually not the disaster that prompts your friend to say, "Someday, we'll laugh about this." You won't. Don't let this friend write a funny memoir.

Even if your memoir is on the heavy side, funny isn't only for people who've had hardship-free lives. Humor is a way to make the tragedy manageable, readable, comprehensible. No matter how serious your story, a little humor can be useful or even necessary. Three hundred pages of unrelenting tragedy will just numb the reader if you don't provide any comic relief. And showing the humor in the situation makes it more well-rounded and real. (Who lives a humor-free existence, after all?) It will also help you get through the writing of it.

Humor is just another implement in your toolbox. It might be for you, and it might not, but it's one more way of telling your story. And if you're pretty sure you're humorless, don't despair. Writing funny is a skill that can be learned, and in this chapter our authors discuss how.

ADVICE FOR THE ASPIRING
COMIC MEMOIRIST

BETH LISICK: Humor is such a bizarre thing. You have to write what makes you laugh. Imagine that you're telling the story to a friend and you really want to make sure they have a good time listening to it. And be prepared to fight to keep what you think is funny in your book. Sometimes it will literally come down to your editor saying, "I don't get it," and you saying, "I'm sorry, but I want to keep it," and her saying, "But it's not funny," and you saying, "Yes, it is."

JONATHAN AMES: I don't know about absolutes, but that old Faulkner line about "killing one's darlings" holds true; in the case of humor, it's usually those things which we feel terribly proud of, proud of our humorous cleverness, and in that case, like an Etch-A-Sketch showing the hidden magnet, the writer's ego is revealed and this is usually a turn-off for the reader.

FIROOZEH DUMAS: You have to decide your boundaries as a humorist. There are certain things I don't touch. I try to be a kind person in life and that includes my writing. Humor can be meanness disguised. I really try not to go there, and instead just find humor in observations that do not hurt anyone. The great thing is that there is a lot of funny stuff out there.

DAVID RAKOFF: I was going to say that it's important you feel comfortable with your writing persona, such as it is, and ask yourself if it has longevity (I've seen more than one young columnist who writes an unbridled column about his or her sexual exploits in their twenties only to disappear so thoroughly it's as though they were killed). Try, first and foremost, to be a writer, without pigeon-holing yourself (others will do it for you soon enough, have no fear). But I don't want to sound all commencement speaker "To Thine Own Self Be True" earnest. So no, nothing. Do whatever. Just remember, the more writing you get under your belt, the better.

DAN KENNEDY: You know, who knows? It's all so subjective. There really aren't any rules. Refrain from making fun of the one person who kicked your ass in the ninth grade. Because it turns out that even if you change the name, they know you're talking about them. When you go home for the reunion, they're waiting for you and they'll kick your ass again. But I have to say that Sandy is an exceptionally strong girl—no shame in her kicking my ass a second time. If I had shoulders like hers, I'd marry her and build us a house.

HOW TO WRITE FUNNY
WITHOUT BEING TOO FLIP

DAVID RAKOFF: Easy. Don't be twenty-three. Forgive me. I take it by this question you mean how to be funny about other people without being flip, correct? It's very important to know what you're going to make fun of and why.

Often the funniest things are simply verbatim reported speech that you don't have to touch at all. Ditto public figures and people who preach one thing publicly but practice the opposite in private. Fair game. If you're making fun of the way someone looks (I mean editorializing beyond mere description) there had better be a good reason for it. Similarly, if you're joking about someone's level of education, privilege, or lack thereof, etc. If you use them, it should be germane to the point you're making.

I break these rules all the time. But I try not to. I also have to say, if you follow these rules, it does make you less funny than you could potentially be, but it strikes me as worth it.

SARAH VOWELL: I don't have much of a problem with being flip or detached if it's funny. That said, I don't really set out to "write funny" per se. I set out to write about something in the least generic way possible and in my case I guess that ends up amusing other people. A lot of what I write is deeply sad but luckily people seem not to remember that. Then again, humor usually derives from sadness and/or outrage.

DAN KENNEDY: I think the biggest thing to make sure of is that whatever humor you're putting on the page, you should be able to just scratch the surface of the "funny" and get to some bigger truth; some core personal stake that we all share as people. I sound like a Sting song right now, but it's true.

I was talking with my friend Catherine Burns last night—she's one of the people behind Stories at The Moth [a not-for-profit storytelling organization] in New York—and she really got me into this theory that having high stakes in a story isn't always a matter of, you know, a bomb on a bus that's going to go off if the bus goes slower than fifty miles an hour or whatever. That there are also these sort of universal set of "personal high stakes" that we all share as human beings; "I want to be loved and this relationship felt like the last shot at it" or "I want my family to see me as an intelligent person" or "I needed to prove to myself that I was finally an adult." On the surface, those stakes seem sort of self-indulgent, but when you stop to consider that we all share certain needs or wants, you realize your story or your humor is admitting that you're just like everyone else.

You want that too. When death, love, loneliness, uncertainty, unrequited ambitions, and things like this are lurking just below the surface of whatever humor you're indulging—that, I think, is when people respond. That little scene in Monty Python's "Holy Grail" speaks volumes if you scratch the veneer.

"Bring out your dead!"

And then the guy they're trying to bring out says, "I'm not dead yet!"

"He says he's not dead."

"Well, he's very ill."

"I'm getting better! I want to go for a walk!"

I mean, that's the day you realize you're ten years older than you were. That's the day you get kicked out of the band, or laid off from a job, that's the day you realize you're not a kid anymore, that's the day you realize your relationship is over, and, yes, that's the day you realize that even if you want to be here forever, life has other plans for you. You've been in that scene a million times, on both sides of the fence. But somebody indulges the dark truth in a funny way, and you're laughing. Hard.

BETH LISICK: It's definitely challenging for me. In my brain, there is an "easy" or "shortcut" humor that can come out if I'm being lazy or not feeling inspired. This is usually the stuff that's more negative or makes me come off looking like a tough guy.

As I edit, I really try to pay attention to the parts of my writing that give me that not-so-fresh feeling. If a cringe even begins to creep in, I axe the line or try to re-word what I'm saying. The goal for me is to reveal something funny without making it look like the punchline to an elaborate set-up.

JONATHAN AMES: Honesty about one's flaws and foibles often leads to humor.

AMY KROUSE ROSENTHAL: I don't know if I ever really set out to be funny, per se. I suppose I do sometimes, for certain things. But more often than not, when I'm writing, I'm not trying to be funny ... I'm trying to be accurate. In *Encyclopedia of an Ordinary Life*, when I'm just observing something, spelling out a moment, like the entry "Stupid Slow Driver" where I'm driving in my car and there is a slow driver and I just have to see what this person looks like because I'm sure he will be stupid looking and in the end my suspicions are confirmed and I drive up alongside him and think "Ah, yes, he looks totally stupid ... he's a stupid, slow driver." Am I trying to be funny here? Not really. But the idea is funny, I guess, because people read it and say "I do that. That's funny." It resonates.

FIROOZEH DUMAS: Writing humor requires a lot of patience. I read and re-read everything dozens of times and will spend hours on one sentence, trying out different versions to see which is the funniest. It's a very detail-oriented process. Sometimes, it turns out that the first way I write something is the funniest, sometimes the twenty-fifth is the keeper.

Chapter X

WRITING THROUGH PAIN

Handling trauma and drama

Memoir is like literary alchemy, a way of transforming your most unpleasant experiences into art. It's tremendously cathartic. Once the pain and embarrassment and guilt are down on the page. It's redemptive: you're the author, the one with agency, and even if you can't change how things turned out, you can change how you feel about them.

By focusing on the lighter events you might be skirting the deeper issues that would make the book better, rounder, more powerful. Maybe not—there may not be a dark side to, say, cheerleading camp—but it's worth exploring.

Writing out the trauma can change your life. It can also change the reader's, letting them know there's someone else in the world who hurt in the exact same way they hurt. It's a brave and generous act.

It is also a delicate business. It can be hard to tackle tough subjects like death, abuse, sickness, or trauma with enough emotion to make it real, but not so much self-pity that it's off-putting or disingenuous. The first draft might be too mawkish, the second, too spare. Keep at it; you'll find the balance.

In this chapter, writers who've experienced all this and more share their methods for getting the hard stuff down. Sure, it's difficult, but you've survived a lot worse. Be brave and charge forward.

HOW TO HANDLE THE DIFFICULT
SUBJECTS WITH A DEFT HAND

NICK FLYNN: Remember that your story is no worse than anyone else's. I haven't met a person yet who couldn't tell me a story that could break my heart, and that makes me feel less alone.

FRANK MCCOURT: Reduce it to simplicity. It's a time when you learn the value of straight talk and to write clear, simple English. You have to cut out any sentimentality. I learned a lot from teaching. You get up there and you're dealing with the most critical people. The thing about them is they want the truth. I decided, as much as possible, as much as I could, to tell the truth, in as straightforward a way as I could.

ART SPIEGELMAN: With *Maus* I had to avoid "Holokitsch," the idea that everything comes complete with violins in the background. In general, if you tamp things down and mute them, they tend to amplify in the reader's eyeball and brain.

I do everything wrong and then I try to fix it. I can get incredibly callous and cool. Or, conversely, I can go into something that's too emotionally fraught and doesn't leave room for the reader's emotion. It's a matter of finding that zone.

JULIA SCHEERES: Don't throw yourself a pity party. Just write the facts and let the reader make her own decision about how she feels about the events/people. Write everything in full-blown color yet in a nuanced fashion. If you write too much poor-me gunk, the reader will balk at it and it will have the opposite effect—it'll just come off as whiny.

SEAN WILSEY: The painful stuff needs to be in there. And with it you don't need that much craft, like you do with more pedestrian material. Told clearly, the story will stand on its own. The hardest thing I wrote about was my mom, how she wanted to kill herself and for me to kill myself with her. The rest of the book I wrote and rewrote, but that particular scene, which was the most painful, was the one I just wrote and then didn't look at for a couple of years.

JANICE ERLBAUM: To keep an emotionally difficult scene from becoming sentimental or uncomfortable for the reader, try to see the humor, or the irony, or the improbable thought/feeling/detail in the scene. You don't have to stop and make a joke, just look for the parts of the scene that are unsentimental, and include some of those. But sometimes you're going to write things that make your readers uncomfortable—that's not always a bad thing.

ANTHONY SWOFFORD: I never worry about making the reader uncomfortable. If I am willing to write it they should be willing to read it and to possibly get uncomfortable.

CAROLINE KRAUS: Finding the appropriate tone is intuitive for me, it just happens during the writing. But usually a neutral voice works to balance the more difficult scenes and prevent tipping toward sentimental or trite.

MATTHUE ROTH: I actually don't know how *not* to deal with the painful parts. I haven't really gotten over it in real life—my best friend dying, couch-surfing for a year, and then getting married halfway around the world from any of my friends—and so the jagged bits of the last three years are still quite jagged. I tried not writing them to be *quite* so painful, or writing them in third person, or copying verbatim the stuff that I had in my diary from that time. But you can't do that. You lose the immediacy, the first-person-ness.

PAUL COLLINS: Unless they're in a full-body cast, not many people suffer every minute of every day. So focusing on only painful experiences, or even primarily on painful ones, makes writing palpably false.

Life is just not like that for most people, even the "tragic" ones. And even when there are painful experiences, I keep my response restrained out of a sense of dynamic tension in a work.

In *Not Even Wrong*, I cry in one—and exactly one—scene in the whole book. It is key to the book, because it expresses a fear I have for my child. If I had broken down at more than one point in the book, the impact would have been diminished.

RACHEL HOWARD: In *The Lost Night*, I didn't do this to the degree that I would now, but just let the reader *feel* events with you, rather than telling them what you felt. Let them see what you saw, hear what you heard, in the way you saw and heard it and they will feel it.

When I showed drafts of certain chapters of my book to my writers' group, they pushed me hard: We want more emotion! This should be more dramatic! Her father just died! Where is the feeling! I didn't listen to them. The truth was that just after my father died I was overwhelmed and numb, and that's what I tried to capture in the writing. If I had taken the advice from my writers' group, the book would have been self-pitying and melodramatic. What I captured is the truth of how I felt, not some retrospective idea about how I should have felt.

HOW TO PROTECT
YOURSELF WHILE WRITING

JANICE ERLBAUM: I'm in therapy, and have been for the past eleven years, so that helps to protect me from the unhappy memories and emotions that arise in writing memoir. I also have a wonderful partner, some close friends, and a very sensitive writers' group. The more trustworthy people you have on your side while writing a memoir, the better.

CAROLINE KRAUS: For me, writing about difficult life moments didn't often become emotional. I was well past the events I was writing about, so I was engaged at a literary level that extended beyond my own feelings. That said, there were a few times that I did start laughing or crying. In those cases I mostly took it as a sign that I was tapping the right tree.

SEAN WILSEY: If you're looking at history, you can wind up reliving it. This can be annoying for the people in your life now. As soon as you start to examine the past, it does have a new life. I would try to shut it out when I wasn't writing, but, inevitably, in terms of emotions or just *conversation*, it would come up.

ART SPIEGELMAN: I wear a bicycle helmet. So when I bang my head against the wall it doesn't hurt quite as much.

ON CATHARSIS

RACHEL HOWARD: The night that I sat down and tried to write what I could remember of [my father's] murder scene was terrifying. I was afraid I couldn't handle what I might remember. And when I got it all down, and didn't have a mental breakdown, I knew I could handle any-thing—it was so freeing.

If something feels "dangerous" to write about, the best thing you can do for yourself is write it. This is pretty standard Post-Traumatic Stress Disorder counseling, but when you write what you remember of an event, you separate yourself from it. You create a new layer of memory on top of the original one—a memory of you being in control of the old memory. You no longer have to relive that memory as though it's happening in the moment every time it gets triggered. The panic dissolves.

Chapter XI

THE FACTS vs.
THE TRUTH

How much license is poetic?

This is, without question, the thorniest issue in memoir, an issue that's become even thornier of late. The thorniness, unfortunately, is inherent. Memoir relies, per the name, on memory, which is notoriously unreliable. It is not biography or resumé, not reportage or diary. On the other hand, it's not fiction. It has to be true. But what, exactly, is true?

In the fine William Zinsser book of the same name, Russell Baker called the memoir process "inventing the truth." In memoir, you do have to take some poetic license. For the sake of readability, time must be collapsed, events elided, dialogue reconstructed. For legal reasons you might have to change names and places. And to convey how powerful something was to you at the time, you may want to heighten the language. But — and here's the rub — you simply can't invent things from whole cloth and call it memoir.

Ultimately, your own memory and conscience will determine what's true. Most publishers don't employ fact-checkers. Most magazines do. This is why memoir excerpts in magazines are sometimes different from the book publisher's version. Someone from The New York Times *or* The New Yorker *has verified every single word. Did the vein in your father's head really throb, or did he just wrinkle his brow? Did your sister call you a "four-star dork" or just a plain unmodified dork? Were you in Prague for your whole junior year or just one semester? Was it really the coldest winter there ever, or did it just feel that way to you?*

It's difficult to write while you're questioning yourself like that, so you'll just have to get it down the way it feels true to you. Afterward you can go back and rework the places where you've taken too much license, gotten carried away by the narrative, strayed too far.

For some writers, sticking to fact is too constraining. Others find it liberating. Nonfiction does let you do some things that would never work in fiction. A scene in Julia Scheeres's Jesus Land *illustrates this perfectly: Young Julia arrives at her Dominican Republic tough-love camp where the staff greets her with smiles and a sign welcoming her by name. Within seconds the staff has stomped the sign into a trash can, foreshadowing the way they'll be treating her in the months to come. That detail would have been overly symbolic if it hadn't really happened, if Scheeres were telling the story as a novel. But it did happen, and it's presented truthfully, and it's perfect.*

You'll find your perfect truths, too. In this chapter, our authors reveal their policies and techniques for finding theirs.

SOME THOUGHTS ON THE ROLE OF TRUTH IN MEMOIR

TOBIAS WOLFF: There's no question that the operations of memory have a great deal of imagination in them. Otherwise we'd all remember things exactly the same way. We're bringing our peculiar sense of the past to bear; each of us is a filter. None of us has an objective view of the past. There are historical events that are verifiable, but the things that we like to get into as writers have to do with character and texture and relationship—these are not objective, measurable insights.

You can see this in family members discussing events of twenty years ago—they always have different versions, sometimes comically so. For instance, I may be the leading character in all my memories, but I'm not the leading character in my friend's memories, who may be offended that he wasn't occupying a more central role in my account of events.

There's always that subjective slant to the act of remembering things. I don't have a problem with that. But when you're intentionally making things up, you have to acknowledge that, and call it fiction. My last book, for instance, is told in the first person, and draws to some extent on certain experiences of mine, but it's a novel and it's called a novel. Anyone who reads it as a memoir does so at his own peril. I made up a lot of what's in there. This is an ancient and holy tradition in writing. You have to know the difference when you're writing and you have to be honest about it.

SEAN WILSEY: I approached my book with the attitude that no cheating was allowed, that I had to write it like a reporter, because I was at *The New Yorker*, and at *The New Yorker* immediately following Janet Malcolm's time in court for cleaning up quotes and resetting scenes. I obviously don't have a transcript of everything that happened to me, but I struggled to make sure every conversation was accurate. I immersed myself, talking to people, revisiting events that were really unpleasant to recall, and reconstructing as accurately as possible.

I can't judge anyone else, and there are different ways to approach it. But since I was writing about someone who would take any opportunity to sue, that pushed me to be extra reportorial. Besides, from a craft point of view, I don't like the idea of playing with stuff—I think it's a great challenge to make a book both alive and as accurate as possible.

FRANK MCCOURT: Most of us have lives filled with interesting things. You don't need to create fiction. Just tell your story, that's all. Hemingway just told his story. It's enough. Everybody's story is enough. If I lived another hundred years, I could write a hundred books about my family, and they could write a hundred books.

LAURA FRASER: Well, this has been getting a lot of ink. I say stick to real events and real time and real content of conversations. Of course, the dialogue is not written the way it came out of someone's mouth, but the key phrases and ideas were there. Memoirs are about memory, and so you write in a way that is as true to your memory as possible. Our memories are tinged with emotion and are always interpreting and can never be mistaken for objective truth. That said, I think if you're going to make shit up, you should call it "fiction."

AZADEH MOAVENI: I bear in mind the question of intent, and sometimes when I need to make a choice of this nature, I project myself into the future and try to imagine whether I'd be able to defend the license I'd taken if someone found out or took offense. If I could make a strong case for what I want to do, I go ahead and do it. Otherwise, I'd find some other way to move that bit of the story along.

STEVE ALMOND: You're allowed (required, actually) to be radically subjective in memoir. But you have to be radically subjective about experiences that objectively took place.

Every narrative is shaped. You don't just write every single thing that ever happened to yourself, or your characters. You choose the ones that push us into compelling danger. That said, you shouldn't knowingly lie in a memoir. You should be aiming at the truth of an emotional experience, but not by contriving actual experiences. Embellishing for humorous effect, sure, fine. Condensing time, okay. Reconstructing dialogue. Yes, if need be. But don't invent, unless you want to write fiction.

SARAH VOWELL: I'm not particularly judgmental about other writers stretching the truth a tad. No one is ever going to remember dialogue word for word, especially if it happened long ago. So just try your best. Obviously, if you're calling your work nonfiction and your truth stretches include, say, erroneously maligning a physician's medical ethics, that's wrong. Personally, I would never combine two characters into one in a work of nonfiction. Nor would I change chronology. I guess if you feel like you must do those things, for Pete's sake, say you're doing it up front. Really, though, the whole reason nonfiction is sort of (to me) more fun to write than fiction is that so many unbelievable things actually happen, whereas fiction has to be somewhat plausible.

DAVID MATTHEWS: Dialogue, sensory details—neither can be recorded faithfully in a memoir, and I'd argue that you shouldn't even try. Describe the events a) as you remember them, and b) as entertainingly as you can. When in doubt, go with b.

As far as documentable events—divorces, births, deaths, etc.—you must do both a and b. That's the hardest part of memoir writing. No matter what, just don't be boring—which is why I think you should have written a lot of other stuff, even just for fun, before you tackle a memoir. Just having a story to tell ain't enough. You've still gotta be a writer at heart.

ELIZABETH GILBERT: You know, I'm surprised by how much untruth people automatically assume is present in any memoir. I got a letter recently from a woman who'd read *Eat, Pray, Love* and she had a small favor to ask—she wanted me to write to her and confess all the parts of the book I had made up.

There was nothing vindictive about her request, she said; she was simply wondering. She didn't *mind* that I had made up so much of my memoir, she assured me; it's just that she was curious to know which parts. She had some ideas. For instance, she was pretty sure I'd made up the bit at the end about falling in love with the Brazilian guy in Bali—that was obviously too good to be true and clearly I had invented it just to manufacture a happy ending. (Meanwhile, I had just married that actual Brazilian the week earlier, after a three-year courtship.)

I don't even know what to do with letters like this, or questions like this, which come up now all the time. Why do people assume that if a story has adventure, coincidence, amazing characters, snappy dialogue, or a happy ending that it all must have been invented, or at least mightily manipulated? I don't get this.

My friend Shea—an artist and traveler—thinks that this new suspicion of true stories speaks to an absence these days of public imagination, or a lack of real-world experience. He told me once, after having traveled around the world for a year and having come back with great stories, which few people believed, "I just say to these people—*you* go travel around the world for a year. You see what turns up."

My memoir is full of coincidence and crazy characters and episodes of almost unbelievable good fortune and happenstance because that's what my *journey* was filled with. The difficult challenge for me, while writing this book, was not trying to figure out how to embellish the truth or invent "interesting" scenes, but how to decide what parts not to tell, because there was so much interesting stuff to choose from. I lived that year full-tilt, and I collected enough real material for a lifetime.

The truth is wild and amazing enough. I don't think it needs much embroidery. Stories need to be *polished*, as I learned growing up in a family of terrific storytellers whose tales got better and better over the years as they figured out how to bring out the best, shiniest, funniest parts of a true anecdote. But they didn't invent those stories. They just cut out the boring parts and highlighted the wonderful parts and perfected their delivery. I learned from childhood that stories don't need to be flat-out invented, not when life is generous already with true wonder, and not when you know how to tell it well.

ANTHONY SWOFFORD: Characters should never be combined in memoir. If you tell the public you have written this memoir, and it is true, you can't go making things up, especially at the level of character. That is a lie; your credibility is gone. If you are combining characters you should probably not be writing a memoir about this particular event, you should just write a novel. The reconstruction of dialogue is obviously a necessary tool. The memoir is not a documentary, and the reader knows this. But you must know these subjects well enough to be able to inhabit their voices and their ethos, to put their words in their mouths. Nor should the writer diverge from factual events. For different people the truth of those events might have been different. *Rashomon* is everyone's favorite example, and a fine one, but the events themselves must not be altered. That is what novels are for. In terms of time, this is why the nonlinear form is my favorite for the memoir—otherwise you are bogged down by, "Five months later Florence and I returned to Costa Rica to see how ... " Bad news.

FIROOZEH DUMAS: This is a sensitive topic for me. I am very angry with writers of nonfiction who lie. It casts a shadow of doubt on everyone's work. A memoir is simply the author's memory. It is understood that dialogue is not verbatim, but an honest recollection. Nothing should be invented. If a conversation did not happen, do not say it did. It's okay to combine characters for the sake of story, as long the characters actually existed.

You can play with the truth, but you can't invent people and events that did not happen. In *Funny in Farsi*, I changed the name of two people, one because I shared a very embarrassing story about him, and the other because I knew she had passed away and I could not locate her family to get their permission, or rather, their blessing. (It was a sweet story but I just wanted to be protective.) Changing their names did not affect the story one bit. The people existed, the events happened. One more detail about memoir writing: I might describe an event as boring but my brother might describe it as thrilling. We're both telling the truth. That's the beauty of a memoir. It's all about one person's perspective. In that sense, the "truth" can seem flexible, but we all know the difference between telling our truth and completely making things up.

BETH LISICK: To be brief, I don't think it's okay to lie on purpose in order to make your story better or more marketable. If you're the only one who knows you're lying, and you can live with that, congratulations.

I often go out of my way so I don't have to make things up. I find the "inventing" of truth very difficult. Not to say I don't elide, combine, and reconstruct because of course I do, but even if I am just describing a sweater someone wasn't wearing, in order to create an image, I think, "I can't believe I just fabricated an outfit someone actually wasn't even wearing!" It makes me feel a little unclean.

ALISON SMITH: Truth is hard. It's harder than it sounds. Just ask your family about a memory you have of them. I guarantee that someone in your family will disagree with your memory. I bet at least one family member will tell you that you got it wrong. They will tell you that things you know in your bones happened didn't ever happen, and vise versa.

Memoirists have only two tools—memory and imagination. They must use both of these tools and they must use them judiciously. I do wish there was some standard, some yardstick we could use to measure the truth factor in a memoir. But such a thing has yet to be invented. In the meantime, writers need to understand the weight of their words. They must honor the people they write about by writing about them with compassion, with candor, with generosity. It's the only decent thing to do. And it makes for a better book. The more nuanced, the more multifaceted, the more empathic you are, the richer the work will be.

JONATHAN AMES: Maybe because I write out my life in small doses—individual events—I don't have to do as much time collapsing or character-melding ... Dialogue, of course, has to be reconstructed. I think that once you start changing events or creating events that didn't happen, it's no longer memoir, but autobiographical fiction.

DAN KENNEDY: I stick with what happened, really. I'm a terrible liar anyway. The truth is always funnier. The bottom line is: I guarantee you that the little, tiny, seemingly benign truths about the way things really happened—the way it all really went down—those are where the best material is. In *Permanent Midnight*, Jerry Stahl doesn't take the time to convince you he was a hardened criminal in his worst moments—he's going to tell you the truth, that story about the dented canned food scam being his big bad-ass criminal moment; and when he tells it, it's brilliant, and sad, and hilarious, and true.

PHILLIP LOPATE: I take the liberty at times to collapse several events into one, to change names or addresses as a way of protecting others, to reconstruct dialogue. Beyond that, I try to tell the truth as much as I can. I like the truth, I prefer the truth to invention. It is not a policy so much as a quasi-mystical belief: that life experience has an underlying form, and that it is the job of the autobiographical writer to find that form. Why invent when the facts are interesting enough, if only one can arrange them properly?

DAVID RAKOFF: Because my training, such as it is, was in magazines that employ fact-checking departments, the policy is to tell the truth and be prepared to back it up. I'm very pleased to say I've never been challenged on that front. But it really depends on the kind of writing you're doing. I like truth, myself (sadly reflected in my book sales, I'm afraid). Obviously events get compressed for the sake of concision, but I really try not to alter the truth of things I choose to put into the story.

GUS LEE: Our extrapolations must be ruthlessly consistent with our understanding of the characters and their times. Otherwise, we've crossed the line into fantasy—a fine country for the pen, but not the one you've declared it to be. I like the theory of writing about what is difficult—to face fear, which is the unique place in which we can meet courage.

PAUL COLLINS: Fiction is fabricated by the author; nonfiction is what is left after the author has cut away materials from the extant world. So nonfiction is necessarily a massive process of omission. That is not the same as fabrication, and it's facile when authors conflate the two. I don't believe in the concept of greater poetic truths. I really don't. It's a convenient lie for dishonest artists.

JANICE ERLBAUM: Be as honest as you can be. You're going to have to leave out stuff that happened, but don't put in stuff that didn't happen. You will have to recreate dialogue, but don't create dialogue. Don't make people say things they never said, or never would say. If you have to change the timeline, try to keep it as close to the actual events as possible. And I've tried compositing characters in order to protect people's identities, but it didn't work—people recognized themselves anyway—so I don't think there's a good reason to do so. Whatever you do to change the story must be acknowledged in an author's note before the text. If you don't feel like being honest about your life, call it fiction.

CAROLINE KRAUS: I think when dealing with facts, a memoir should be scrupulously true and vetted. And when dealing with feelings, perspectives, and memories, which extend from those facts, readers should understand that subjective truth is operating. Some of the techniques used to bring both objective and subjective facts alive include dialogue, scene description, and time manipulation. It's not too complicated.

TANYA SHAFFER: A memoir is not journalism. It's a personal essay based on memory, which everyone knows is unreliable. It's a trip inside an individual's head, to look at that person's experiences through his or her eyes. I think it's perfectly acceptable to combine insignificant characters and trivial events for the sake of advancing the story. If you had to keep every tiny detail in line it would be so boring that no one would read it.

Having said that, we have to acknowledge the fact that a memoir is not being sold as fiction. That means that larger events and people can't be invented out of whole cloth. In my view, you have to stay true to the basic events, but it's okay to manipulate details to make it possible for the reader to experience the essence of the tale more clearly.

AMY KROUSE ROSENTHAL: I think you just do your best. Unless we could put a wire into the brain and there was some computer program that could turn your memory into words, it's a really tricky, difficult thing. If you're a writer, and if your intent and your integrity are there, I think that counts for a lot.

The fact is, we all remember things differently. It's like *Rashomon*, the same story told four different ways, four people remembering the same incident differently yet they can all be considered versions of the truth. It's fascinating. How do you account for that? How do a household of people, of siblings and parents, for instance, remember the exact same events differently? In *Encyclopedia of an Ordinary Life*, I worked really hard to make dates accurate—and in cases where there was recorded data, it was factual. But in cases where I was tracing a memory, like in the childhood memories section, for instance, I just did my best to map it all out. If I was a little off, I hope readers will forgive me. Memoir writers are not journalists; we're not reporting "facts." We're trying our best to grab at that elusive stuff of our lives and record it honestly.

TAMIM ANSARY: I'm sort of dogmatic. You can't make things up, because then it's not a memoir. For me, the premise is that the original story-like essence is actually there, and I am very committed to that. When you start changing things to make it a better story, you lose that.

I was at this memoir workshop and another memoirist there made an interesting point that clarified things for me. He said of course you make up stuff in a memoir. But you do that to recreate the truth as you know it. It's a different thing when you make up stuff because you want to glorify yourself or create a truth that wasn't there. When I went to Afghanistan people told me stories that were difficult to repeat—they were too horrible. At some point I started thinking they weren't factual. But I think they were telling me that to give me a sense of how painful the events really had been for them. It made it more lurid, so I could feel how they felt when the thing happened.

ART SPIEGELMAN: Well, the nature of comics involves reconstruction. In *Maus*, I couldn't fit in all the language that was in my father's tapes. So it has to be turned into a shortened version. The nature of comics in general, and of writing in general, is to create concision. So what you're left with is a fractal of what was there. After that it's a matter of sifting to "figure out"—big quotes—what objectively would be true.

The main thing I know is that when I do something that is genuinely fiction I have trouble because it's like playing tennis without a net. It's too arbitrary.

When I have something that is genuinely true then I can feel free to lie with impunity, because it's all a matter of trying to get to the truth.

Chapter XII

LOST IN THE LABYRINTH

Substance-free cures for stasis

Standstills are a normal part of the writing process. It's like anything else—work followed by rest. You need to get stuck sometimes, to give your brain a chance to catch up. It's a mandatory vacation; you can make good use of the time off by reading, exploring, refilling your mind. A period of rest—or even block—can take the manuscript in a new and better direction. It makes you approach from different angles, mine for new material, try new methods. Then you'll come back to the book with fresh eyes, and you'll know what needs editing. A cake that's been sitting out for a while is easier to cut. So is a manuscript.

HOW TO MOVE FORWARD
WHEN YOU'RE BLOCKED

ELIZABETH GILBERT: First of all, with forgiveness and compassion. Forgive yourself that you are having trouble and show yourself some compassion that you have disappointed yourself in your work. There is so much talk in the writing world about the importance of discipline, but I truly think forgiveness and compassion are more important qualities. Discipline is hard, rigid, mean, and forceful. Most of us don't have it. Or at least we don't always have it.

Everyone makes vows and promises—*I will write ten pages of my novel every day*—and everyone falls short of those vows. The writers who keep writing are the ones who get up every day and instead of beating themselves up—*I'm a failure, I'm useless, I have no discipline*—go back to their desk and, with great forgiveness and compassion, try again.

Also—not every story needs the same thing from you, so you have to be flexible and responsive. Creativity is a living force. It exists in the heavens and wants to come through you—the hardworking human—in order to be actualized on earth. But each story has a different character. Some stories need to be bullied—you have to force them to come through, showing that you are as strong as they are, or stronger. Other stories need to be seduced—you have to gently convince them that it's safe to be told. If you hate your story, resent your story, get angry at your story, it will sometimes retreat forever. So the hardness of discipline itself isn't enough. You need faith and patience and love in order to attract creativity.

Also—bribes work sometimes. (I tell myself at times, "If you write three pages today, I'll take you to the movies tonight.") But, as any parent can tell you, empty threats mean nothing ...

DAVID RAKOFF: I'm terrible at this. Truly, I need deadlines and someone else enforcing them. Panic is my most effective tool. Otherwise it's me and the Kettle Krinkle Cut Salt and Black Pepper chips.

JANICE ERLBAUM: I find that block happens for three reasons. One major cause of block occurs when you're too emotionally close to the events you're writing about. If this is true for you, then you've either got to stop working on this project and let some time pass, or talk frankly with someone you trust about your feelings until you feel more resolved.

Another big reason for block is not knowing where to start. In which case, forget about where to start—just jump into the middle of the story (or even the middle of the scene), and go back and fill in the beginning later. A third cause of block is when you've written yourself into a corner—you just love that one scene or paragraph or line you wrote, but it doesn't let you flow into the next scene or paragraph or line. This is when you have to go back and take out the thing you loved so much and put it in your "scraps" folder, for possible use later. It's so hard to scrap something you're crazy about, but if you find that you can't seem to move on, it's probably because it's not serving the story.

FRANK MCCOURT: I hear a lot about writer's block. I remember what Steve Martin said, that writer's block is just an excuse to go out and get drunk, and you don't need to do that at seven o'clock in the morning. I don't believe in writer's block, anyway. You don't hear about that on the other side of the Atlantic Ocean, only in America. You think about a writer like Anthony Trollope who would get up and write 3,000 words, and then go off to his job as a postal inspector. And I believe Sinclair Lewis used to write 5,000 words every day. That's an awful lot of words.

AZADEH MOAVENI: I just glue myself to my seat and stick with the discomfort until it passes. I also make a point of reading more during times of blockage. I find that exposing myself to the voices of authors I enjoy or take inspiration from usually unsticks me.

PHILIP LOPATE: I write something else—an article, a diary entry, a book review. I am rarely stuck, to be frank. But some pieces take longer to write than others, and I am patient in giving them as much time as they seem to need.

TANYA SHAFFER: Any time I'm having trouble I go back to freewriting. I fool myself, just as I did writing papers in college, by telling myself that this isn't the real thing: I'm going to write something now that no one will ever read, just to get my hands moving. I tell myself I'm just writing the story down to get it clear in my head, and then I'll worry about working on my "actual" draft. Then I give myself ten, fifteen, twenty minutes and say "go," and the only rule is my fingers don't stop moving. (I owe this technique to Natalie Goldberg's *Writing Down the Bones*.) Once I've gotten myself going, I generally don't want to stop.

NICK FLYNN: Since I try to make writing a daily practice, I don't really get blocked. I write a lot of garbage, but I don't get blocked.

AMY KROUSE ROSENTHAL: I feel like writer's block is a clichéd term that is not exactly right for what happens to me. But if something isn't flowing, if it's just not feeling right, then I close that file on my laptop and switch gears and work on something else. Now, if you're a novelist and all you're doing is working on one novel and it's not jiving, that would be really difficult. I guess that could be considered writer's block. But if you are an artist who is open to the idea of going to your computer or your canvas or your pottery wheel and simply letting whatever wants to come forth that day come forth, I think you are then minimizing your chances of this so-called writer's block.

Sometimes I find I have this essay I'm working on for a magazine and it's just not coming together and everything is terrible but, at the same time, I'm thinking about this one sentence and maybe that will turn into an idea for a children's book, or a gift book. Basically, if I'm blocked in one place, it means I should be in another place.

LAURA FRASER: I make myself write. I carve out two hours and sit there and work on something. Maybe I throw it away, but I'm working. When I have a project going, I give myself manageable, bite-sized deadlines, so I don't freak out about having so much to do. That said, I've been pretty blocked about writing another book for awhile. I'm in a bit of a sophomore slump.

DAN KENNEDY: Make phone calls, take a walk, watch a movie—sit with it long enough and you move on.

JONATHAN AMES: Reasonable goals made even more reasonable—I will sit at my desk for thirty minutes. Literally, just sit there and if I jot something down, on a pad, or on the computer, then great. Early on, I learned that you can't write a whole book in one day, but if you have that mind set, you won't even get started.

Also, reading writers I love inspires me—I want to try to write the sentences they write, tell the kinds of stories they tell.

ANTHONY SWOFFORD: I read. I think about steak. I do other things that can't be mentioned in a family publication.

A.J. JACOBS: I do sometimes just start writing. It doesn't matter what. It's not the content so much as the feeling of clicking those silver keys on my Mac. So I'll write about the pigeon on my window sill, or the fact that my orange juice glass is dirty. Anything at all. Just to get the fingers moving.

FIROOZEH DUMAS: Take a hot bath, or get a good night's sleep. If I feel like my tires are stuck in the mud, I have to remove myself from the story and go back to it later. It never ceases to amaze me how obsessive I can be sometimes when all I really need to do is let go and revisit the story later.

STEPHEN ELLIOTT: I sit and eat potato chips and get fat and complain that I'll never write again, and then I do.

Chapter XIII

THE END OF YOU (FOR NOW)

Concluding your memoir

Ending a book is always difficult, but with a memoir, it's also strange: you're still alive, your story is ongoing, and your perspective on the past is ever-changing. No matter what, you're jumping off a train that's still in motion.

There are dozens of different ways to wrap up a book. Your ending can be hopeful, absurd, tidy, messy, definite, or vague. You can tie up the loose ends or unravel them. You can end with a bang or a whimper.

Enjoy this part. Savor it. Writing the conclusion is the most satisfying bit of the whole process. When you finally figure out that last paragraph, you'll feel so smug and giddy it will be hard to type.

You might even be a little choked up. Endings can be wistful. Maybe you're having a good time and you don't want to leave the party, maybe you have a fear of closure. Either way, it helps to remember it's never really goodbye—you can always revise, always write an epilogue (or a sequel).

It's the final sprint after a long marathon. You're almost there, and we're running out of metaphors, so we'll turn you over to the experts and let you finish.

HOW TO FIND YOUR ENDING

JANICE ERLBAUM: The book ends when you've either reached your original goal, abandoned your original goal, or gotten a new goal. Sometimes it ends with a major life event—graduating from the Air Force academy, or getting married, or getting divorced, or attending the premiere of your first movie, and sometimes it will end with a major revelation—realizing that your dead grandfather will always live in your memory, or that you're not in love with the guy you thought you were going to marry after all. The book ends when you've finished one phase of your life—when you've gone through a major change, and are ready for your next major change.

CAROLINE KRAUS: I think you know you've reached the end when you've answered the questions that got the story moving at the beginning, and when you've made sense of the experience for yourself.

JAMES MCMANUS: Write three or four and try to gauge which one has the sense of an ending. I often take elements of two or three possible endings and combine them into one.

STEVE ALMOND: I rewrote the ending of *Candyfreak* at least three times. The key is recognizing a passage, or an image, that feels like the end, not trying to contrive some big, phony crescendo. That kind of staginess never works.

FRANK MCCOURT: In the beginning, when I wrote *Angela's Ashes*, I was going to write a bigger book. I was going to bring it all the way up to my teaching days—he's born in America, he goes back to Ireland, he returns to America and joins the army, he teaches for thirty years. I was going to do all of that, but I just went to age nineteen, to coming back to America. It seemed complete, with a beginning, middle, end.

None of it is instinct. Who knows where it comes from.

TOBIAS WOLFF: You're looking for patterns in your past, looking for a larger pattern. When you feel that the pattern has been completed, then the book is over. Not everyone is satisfied with that—I've had readers express disappointment that I didn't continue the narrative. But it's called *This Boy's Life*—when the boy's life is over, then the era of permitted irresponsibility is over, and when that's over, the book's over. When he goes out, he's on his own—his mistakes, he'll have to pay for. It's that sort of instinct that guides me in form. Others may have other lights that they follow, but that's mine.

JONATHAN AMES: The ending, at some point, comes to you. It's artistic grace. Same thing with the ends of essays. At some point, you hit on what you realize is your ending.

DAN KENNEDY: It's that moment when you go to yourself, "Whoa. This is the end, isn't it?" You've had the feeling before, and you'll recognize it in an instant.

DAVID RAKOFF: When to end: once the Mother Wolf has gnawed off her own foot to save her cubs and the snow surrounding the steel trap is scarlet with blood. That's a tough question to answer and I'm afraid the only one I can give is that maddening "How will I know if I'm in love?" response, which is, "You'll know." Endings, almost more than any other part of a story, seem to have an embedded canary in the mineshaft that starts squawking and dying when a false epiphany or unearned resolution is being tacked on. Luckily for me, hack that I am, I have trained myself to be impervious to the strangled death rattle of said birds ...

BETH LISICK: For *Everybody Into the Pool*, the story of taking my son to a baby massage class seemed like a natural ending. Even though he was a couple years old by the time I wrote the book, and there were many more stories I could tell, parenting-related and otherwise, that story felt right because it seemed like both an end and a beginning. I like that in a book. An ending that seems like a whole new chapter is about to begin.

LAURA FRASER: For me, the story naturally ended—the affair was over, things had changed, I'd been delivered from one shore to the other. I wrote a little coda on the end that was hopeful and also left people hanging. I don't want to tie things up too perfectly. It always surprises me when people ask (as they do several times a week) whether my love affair with the professor is still continuing, if I still see him. I thought it was obvious that it was over. Otherwise I would've ended with us moving to India together or something.

RACHEL HOWARD: My story ended with a wedding, which is a traditional source of resolution, and fortunately in my case that wedding arrived with much genuine resolution about facing my father's death. It was a false ending, though, in that I depicted the wedding as being ecstatic perfection, everything set right in my life, and in fact I was uneasy about that wedding and ended up divorcing my husband. My publishing house put pressure on me to emphasize getting married as a frame for the story. I think that aspect is the only fake thing in a book that is otherwise thoroughly honest.

NICK FLYNN: Part of writing the book, it turned out, was developing a relationship with my father, something I hadn't had before (a Jungian might say that this was the unconscious reason I was writing the book), but at some point I did have to decide on the endpoint of this, how I would present this relationship, which is still transforming. Part of how I did that was by making a decision, at some point, to start the book with the word "please" and to end it with the word "generous," which created a container for me to work within. The word "generous" is part of something my father said at one moment, and this forced me to end the book on that moment.

ANTHONY SWOFFORD: You should never start a memoir without knowing *where* the book ends; not necessarily how, but you must know where, in the treacherous timeline of your life, the story ends. That is one of the bonuses of memoir! For me, my major start and end points were going to war and returning. Then I had to fill it all in.

DAVID MATTHEWS: This gets us right back to theme. If your story was the (admittedly lame) one I described earlier, about the boy who falls in love with his older stepsister, the end of the story is probably some variety of when the boy finds a girl his own age, or when he marries his stepsister twenty years later. That theme is forbidden love—the end of the story is that point at which the love is either realized or abandoned by the narrator. As the writer, you get to pick the moment which best illustrates the answering of the question you posed at the beginning of the book: "Will our hero find love?" etc.

A.J. JACOBS: It doesn't have to be a big explosion there at the end. My Bible book ends with a quiet dinner with my family. As long as you've taken the reader on a transformational journey, you don't have to wrap everything up with a bow like a sitcom.

FIROOZEH DUMAS: I have only written one book ... but at some point, I felt I was done for that book. I never looked back. I am surprisingly un-obsessive about endings because I feel like there are no endings, just pauses. There is always another story waiting to be told and they are all connected.

Chapter XIV

GETTING IT OUT THERE

Agents, editors, publishers, and lessons learned

Your memoir is done. This bears repeating: your memoir is done. *Your first assignment is to take yourself out to dinner. You must overindulge, order dessert, stay out too late. Tomorrow you'll sleep in, and over breakfast in bed you can decide what to do next. You might want to learn how to solder. You might want to write another book. Or you might want to publish this one.*

You certainly don't have to. Maybe you just wrote it for you, or your family, or posterity. And in that case, your next project is to continue basking in the glory of a job well done. On the other hand, you've put a lot of work into the manuscript, so if you're inclined, it may be worth floating it out into the world to see what happens.

In this chapter our authors tell you what to do now that your memoir is finished: how to find an outlet for publication (newspapers, magazines, books); how to get an agent, if you're so inclined; how to handle rights for movie and TV adaptations (might as well cover that, as unlikely as it is for most); and how to cope once it's out in the world.

HOW OUR AUTHORS FOUND
THEIR PUBLISHERS . . .

JANICE ERLBAUM: When I finished the first draft, I put a query on Publisher's Marketplace (*publishersmarketplace.com*), and some editors saw it and contacted me. None of them bought the book, but one of them was extremely helpful to me—he advised me to start over by writing a proposal, rather than writing a second draft, and he introduced me to the woman who became my agent. Once my proposal was finished, my agent was able to sell the book within six weeks. I am extremely grateful to this editor, and to my wonderful agent.

STEVE ALMOND: Three or four agents turned it down. They thought it was too weird, couldn't figure out where Barnes & Noble would put it in their stores, whatever. So I sent it out myself. Most editors rejected it. But one said yes. And that's all it takes: one.

BETH LISICK: My agent sent me on a bunch of appointments to meet editors in New York. It would best be depicted in a montage scene with some kicky music. The writer! In the big city! Going up and down elevators! Smoothing out her bangs with a quick swipe of the hand as the doors open! What I heard most was that they liked the sample chapters okay, but they didn't think their bosses would buy it. The Man took the blame. In the end, only one publisher made an offer and that was ReganBooks.

LAURA FRASER: Weird story: I had mentioned the idea of the book to my agent, who was not keen on it at first. She then went to the Frankfurt Book Fair, where her German sub-agent asked if she had any authors doing travel. She remembered my idea, which was based on a few travel pieces I'd written already, and called me from Germany asking me if I could have the proposal done by the next day, which I did. The Germans bought it, and then a publishing house in the U.K. followed suit. Then the Dutch. Finally, my agent sent it around in the U.S. Pantheon made a pre-emptive bid, before the auction, and while the money wasn't that impressive, it was a truly wonderful editor. My agent rightly suggested that it was far better to go with a great house and great editor than to get a little bit more money at auction.

STEPHEN ELLIOTT: My first books were submitted blindly to the slush pile. I published five out of my six books without an agent. Though I don't recommend it.

DAN KENNEDY: I did a lot of spoken word gigs, telling the stories that wound up being the stories in the book. For example, there's Stories at The Moth, and there was this thing called "Reading It" for a while downtown at the Luna Lounge. So, basically I was out there doing this sort of thing and I would meet people after the gig. I met a writer named Joshua Wolf Shenk—that was maybe eight years ago, and we've become friends over the years. I write humor and he writes about depression, so we obviously hit it off. But the first thing he said to me was that he had an agent he wanted to refer me to. That started the process of working with the agent about how the proposal should be, what the book could be about, all that stuff. Then we submitted it, there were plenty of rejections—nobody ever really tells you about that part—and then a couple places made a move on it and put offers on the table. But, you know, both books I've sold have been the same process for me: somewhere around thirteen or fourteen rejections, and then all of a sudden two or three publishers make an offer and within a week everything goes crazy and you have to make a decision one afternoon.

CAROLINE KRAUS: An author-friend read what I was writing, suggested I contact her agent, and her agent took me on and found my editor.

TANYA SHAFFER: A small but excellent publisher expressed interest in my book before it really existed, based on knowledge of my work as a solo performer. That interest was a major factor in motivating me to finish the book. When I finally finished it, I showed it to that small publisher, and they were enthusiastic about publishing it. I almost went with their offer, but an inner voice said that after all the work I'd done on this manuscript I owed it to myself to at least try for a bigger publisher that could pay me more money and perhaps help the book find a wider audience. I got an agent and for several months we had no offers. The deadline for giving an answer to that small, excellent publisher was fast approaching. My agent called the two larger publishers who still hadn't responded and told them I was primed to take this other offer unless something else came in within the next week. The day before my answer was due, I had two more offers. One of them was from Vintage, whose travel series, Vintage Departures, I'd always admired and dreamed of one day being a part of.

ANTHONY SWOFFORD: Out of my graduate program at Iowa I had representation with an agent. She sent out the first sixty pages of *Jarhead* {published by Scribner} and three publishers were interested. I went with the house that Hemingway built.

MATTHUE ROTH: I just kept showing my manuscript to everyone who asked, and then a publisher said "yes." Agents are just people with mouths and smooth, non-sweaty handshakes. You can be a person with a mouth, too. Just carry around a handkerchief in your pocket.

...AND HOW YOU CAN FIND YOURS

JANICE ERLBAUM: Start by writing a proposal! I recommend two great books about proposal writing: Eric Maisel's *The Art of the Proposal*, and Susan Rabiner and Alfred Fortunato's *Thinking Like Your Editor*. A proposal will not only help you sell the book, it will help you write the book. I also recommend that aspiring memoirists suck up to whatever authors or famous people they might come in contact with—getting a blurb [an endorsement] from someone famous will help you sell your book.

ELIZABETH GILBERT: Send your work out there into the world, as one friend of mine said, "Like freaking Christmas cards." Just send, send, send. I sent my work out for years before anyone bought it. If the pain of rejection is too much, do what two writer-friends of mine did—they sent each *other's* manuscripts out into the world, so that they could read each other's rejection notes. That way, neither woman had to see her own rejections, but the work was still circulating out there.

But try to make your pitches are personal as possible. Agents and editors know when somebody has just plugged their name into a general database, or have written a letter that essentially reads: "Dear Stranger—I have no idea who you are, but please buy my book." Do your research first. Find out who publishes the authors you most admire, or the genre of book you have just written. Then send a letter reading, "Dear Ms. Jones—I am a great fan of your client Betsy McBook. I also have written a memoir, similar in a way to Betsy McBook's memoir, but based in Iowa, instead of Texas. I hope you can take the time to read my manuscript. If you like Betsy McBook's writing I think you may like mine. And I see that you also represent Henry O'Word, so I know you aren't afraid of unconventional story lines!" Don't send completely inappropriate material to agents or editors who would never publish it. (For instance, your erotic science fiction novel might not be the best match for a well-known children's book publisher.) Doing some research and making your pitches personal will save you time and postage in the end, and will increase your chances.

The other thing is this—I seem to be having a lot of conversations these days with writers who are hoping to find agents or publishers for books they have yet to write, but would like to maybe write some-day, but not without a book advance or some sort of promise from the publishing world. For reasons I hope I don't have to explain, it's un-likely that any publisher would give a hearty book advance to someone who had never written (or finished) a book. At some point you have to actually write the thing, whether somebody is waiting for it or not. Mark Twain once said something like: "Everyone wants to be a writer, but nobody wants to write." I wrote for years and years without any promise that anything would ever come of it. I've only had two careers in my life—unpublished writer, and published writer. I loved the work both ways, though I'm thrilled, of course, to now make my living from it. But I wrote for years because I had to, and I think if you want to be a writer, you almost can't have a choice about it. If it feels like "wasted time" to you to write something which may never be published, then maybe writing isn't your great love? Because at the beginning of any great love story, somebody always has to take a big risk.

A.J. JACOBS: I had no idea how to find an agent. I sent about seventy letters to a bunch of agents in Writer's Marketplace and one of them called me back. This isn't the most efficient way to go. As with any business, it's all about connections. If you have even the most distant connection to an agent—he's the friend of a friend of your mom's optometrist—that's the best method.

JONATHAN AMES: Get published in lit mags, and agents will come to you, or you can use the published piece as a good calling-card for getting an agent. Just send your stuff to lots of magazines—print or Internet. The more you put out there, the more comes back to you.

ANTHONY SWOFFORD: I think the summer writing programs are beneficial. I've taught at them and there are usually agents and editors attending, giving talks, and looking for talent. Editors and agents love nothing more than discovering new talent. All that their old writers do is give them a hard time! Also, the literary quarterlies are a good place to be discovered.

PAUL COLLINS: Shotgunning proposals to the maximum number of people is actually worse than doing nothing, because it won't work and you'll get needlessly demoralized. Look for authors you admire, and find out who their agents are. Look for magazines whose work you like, and find out who the editor is. Those are *your people*, both aesthetically and commercially: they are the ones who you need to be talking with.

BETH LISICK: The good news is that there are as many stories about finding an agent as there are authors with books. There's no one way to do it right. For me, I just kept working and writing and performing, doing the things I loved, until someone came to me. It sounds like a passive approach, but it didn't feel like it because I was busy doing what I liked to do. Publishing houses and agents like people who have proven they can get a lot done on their own.

TANYA SHAFFER: If you've got any writer-friends, former teachers, etc, who'd be willing to refer you to their agent, try that first. Agents get a lot of cold inquiries—any personal connection makes a huge difference in terms of getting your stuff looked at in a timely way.

ALISON SMITH: Protect yourself. I waited until I had gone through eighteen drafts (which took six years) before I started looking for an agent. In that time I worked any number of odd jobs, from dishwasher to pet-sitter to office manager in an art school, to make ends meet. I followed that one rule of bookkeeping for writers: Keep a low overhead. It wasn't until I reached the eighteenth draft that I felt I was ready to put the book into the marketplace. For that's what agents do, they evaluate your writing with an eye for the commercial marketplace. Agents can do a lot of other things. They can be wonderful editors, inspiring advisors, great champions and protectors, but the bottom line is that to keep afloat they have to acquire manuscripts they can then sell to editors. You have to be ready for this sort of commercial feedback when you send your book out.

MATTHUE ROTH: My more well-regarded friends tell me this is wrong, but publish everywhere you can. Even if it's a page. Even if it's a paragraph. Somewhere, someone will see you and think your story's worth telling. More of your story than you've already told. I did a reading in a gay men's bathhouse, and one of the other performers was asked to do a book for a publisher, and he said that he was too busy but there was this cute little straight boy that could write good, why not ask him? And they did.

SOME THOUGHTS ON FILM

ANTHONY SWOFFORD: Go with the producer on a three-speed bike, not the guy driving an Aston Martin. I was lucky in that all of the central people involved with the film of my book were very talented, and moral, and nice. This will never happen again. But they really cared about my book, and they took care with all aspects of the adaptation. Also, it was totally weird. I'm a big fan of the film. But, in the end, no big deal. It's just a movie. The book is mine; the movie is not.

STEVE ALMOND: It's something that might happen, but it probably won't. Don't think about it. And if it does happen, collect whatever money they throw you and stay away from the rest of the process, which, as far as I can tell, involves bullshit and feathers.

A.J. JACOBS: I was lucky enough to have both of my books optioned for movies. God knows if they'll ever be made. But Hollywood is still looking for those high concept ideas—you know, the ones that can be summarized in a single sentence. "Man reads encyclopedia and goes insane."

JONATHAN AMES: It can be very dispiriting. As Pauline Kael said of Hollywood: "You can die of encouragement."

DAN KENNEDY: I had one offer to option my first book. Which seemed like a big deal at the moment, but I don't know if the guy was drunk, or didn't speak English, or maybe he was typing on a Blackberry from the back of a dirt bike, or something—but the whole email was so frantic and it was missing letters and everything. It was like: "Mr. Kennedy, I was love this loser going first! I have direct film suchas there will be an opportunity to talk and would direct it and write the screen. It is an awesome book NO LOSERS! Okay. Let's get touch thru channels." Figured that was probably a pretty good situation to say "no thanks" to.

ELIZABETH GILBERT: People have asked me if I'm afraid that the movie will ruin the book. But the movie *can't* ruin the book—only because the book is finished, completed, its own solid being. The movie can only ruin the movie. But I'm not even so worried about that. I like seeing how creativity works, how stories spread and grow from medium to medium. I don't want to block that process. I want to let the story be whatever it wants to be next, and I think it'd be interesting to see what this becomes, in movie form.

Also, I'm always a little surprised when writers sell their books to Hollywood and then criticize the results. I think when it comes to selling things, you must be willing to let it go, or not sell at all. Trying to hold onto "control" of the product can be exhausting and useless; so many voices are involved in making a film that even the director often can't totally control what a film becomes. Complaining about what Hollywood did to your book is sort of like selling your house to somebody and then driving past it for years, complaining about what the new owners did to the place. ("Geez—that pergola is *awful*!") It's not yours anymore, not in that form. You have to let it go, or don't bother. This book has been nothing but good to me, and nothing will ever change the goodness that it brought. Whatever comes next is just a fun and peculiar bonus, as far as I can see.

FRANK McCOURT: First of all, I was flattered that Hollywood would want to make a picture of this epic of poverty. They were very courteous, they invited me to the opening, so I was touched and flattered. And it's a very strange feeling to sit in a theater and see your life up there on the screen. And then the whole family sees it, your children and grand-children—it's a very powerful experience, especially when it's about your own life.

BETH LISICK: A huge cliché, but a lot of people in that business love to talk a big game and blow smoke up your ass. If I only had a chocolate torte for every time someone was going to adapt something of mine for the big or little screen, we could put on a cakewalk. And by that I mean: Film rights still available. Call me.

THE AFTERMATH:
WHAT TO DO ONCE IT'S OUT
IN THE WORLD

ELIZABETH GILBERT: It's been an interesting experience, now that the book is out there in the world, to see what self-exposure means. I meet people who say, "I feel like I already know you, after reading your book." In point of fact—they do. Or rather—they sort of know me. They know very well the person who I was at the time I wrote the book, as I was living those experiences.

But that was already years ago—and a lot has happened in those years. I've altered with time as we all do. I doubt I'll ever be so self-revealing on the page again, if only because now I'll be self-conscious about it. And also, I've become more private in the last few years—not least of all because of this book. I don't regret showing so much of my-self; the story called for it, but also I see now that my journey, while deeply personal, was also awfully similar to many people's journeys, and readers are finding that the book is not just a doorway into my being, but a mirror reflecting their own. That wasn't my intention—I told this story to save my own life, not to save anyone else's life—but it's a wonderful side benefit that people are using the book now to know themselves better.

MATTHUE ROTH: It's hard. Try to be alone as little as possible, especially if you go on tour. Keep in contact with friends, people who know you; bring one along, if you can. Just to remind you that this book isn't the sum total of your life work. Some nights are huge ego-boosters; other times, you'll travel ten hours, nobody will show, and it'll make you feel like there's no purpose to any of this. There's a purpose. Somewhere, in some bookstore, someone you don't know is reading a page of your book. That's the greatest thing in the world. You're actually communicating with your writing.

STEPHEN ELLIOTT: The worst is that you probably won't make as big a splash as you would like. It's tragic that so many people are less happy after they've been published than they were before. If this is what you want to do, then make a commitment to yourself to be happy when you reach your goal.

AZADEH MOAVENI: Strangely enough, I found myself deeply uninterested in talking about myself while on tour. I had written the memoir, purged myself in the process, and was just so over the issues that had seemed so compelling to me before. I had moved on, and my audience was still interested in the me-in-the-memoir. This gave me real pangs, because I felt that perhaps the whole process had been instrumental, and that I had somehow inflicted my memoir on people when really it was a private exercise. But I remembered in the end that much of my story was universal, that that's why people were responding, and that I could also re-direct their attention to the themes I was still very much engaged with. That helped.

JAMES MCMANUS: Keep your expectations *low*. Most books disappear from the culture in a couple of weeks. To expect much more attention than that will set you up to be disappointed.

BETH LISICK: Try to limit your self-Googling and Amazon rank-checking. I don't mind when someone doesn't like my stuff, if it's not their idea of a good book, but the vicious comments used to really bum me out. Try to develop a thick skin about that stuff and remember that you are probably one of the few people in the world reading about yourself on someone else's blog.

JONATHAN AMES: Just try to be grateful. At some point, the writer's goal was to write the book and then get it published. Anything that happens after that is icing on the cake.

DAN KENNEDY: You kind of can't think about it. I mean, start tugging on that thread and everything comes apart. Also, my book was reviewed pretty widely, and it did okay in sales, but it wasn't mayhem of any sort—it came out in China and that was kind of a trip. That feels strange. It's like, how do you have any idea what this got turned into in translation? A Chinese journalist wrote the foreword, and for all I know he's going, "Here's the story of a man who decided to live his life as a woman after his parents invented uranium and convinced him at an early age that he was the offspring of aliens, and that he would need to be a woman developing real estate into airports and condominiums if he wanted to stay on earth ..."

DAVID RAKOFF: To paraphrase Dan Savage in his brilliant defense of gay parents and their carefully thought-out decision to adopt, no one gets drunk and inadvertently publishes a memoir (hello blogosphere!). I don't feel exposed in that I-went-to-school-naked way, particularly. Being reviewed in general takes some steeling of the nerves, but it's the nature of the beast. It makes one a better, or more fair, writer.

JANICE ERLBAUM: It was very hard, at first, to confront the idea that people were going to be privy to my most embarrassing, shameful, ugly, stupid behaviors. I didn't want my eighty-five-year-old next-door neighbor to read about all the sex I had and the drugs I did! But she did read about it, and she told me that I should never be embarrassed of my past, because it made me who I am today. I'm proud of the person I am today, if not of the person I was back then, and that helps. But it's still hard—every time I hear from someone who knew me back then, and they say they read the book, I cringe a little, thinking of the things they learned about me. I wish you could publish a memoir with the caveat that certain people would never read it, but you can't. My only advice is that you *not* think about this while you're writing the book—worry about it later.

CAROLINE KRAUS: The ups and downs of sales, and the attendant insecurities that go with having such a personal book out can be nerve-wracking, but overall it's only brought good things my way. I cope with the roller coaster by briefly, privately, screaming my head off and then getting back to work.

PAUL COLLINS: It's thrilling and frightening, and the first time you accidentally notice a copy of your book in a bookstore window is always a stunning moment.

I do find that it helps to have already moved on to another project by the time your book comes out: it puts things in perspective. Also, the people who actually get a book generally don't feel the need to tell the author about it—so don't take public reaction or reviews as particularly representative of your book's meaning or fate.

FIROOZEH DUMAS: I love that people feel like they know me. I love that people relate to my stories. It's all been good.

ART SPIEGELMAN: In some ways *Maus* was both the culmination of all I could have hoped for and the greatest calamity that could have happened to me. On the other hand it's just made it much more difficult for me to work. It's hard to get the eyeballs off my shoulder.

After X number of years you just say: I've got to do it. It's a lot easier to be a genius when no one's calling you one.

ANTHONY SWOFFORD: Never think about this eventuality when you are writing. It will poison you. Pretend that no one will ever read your book. And then when it's out … I don't know, forget about it again. Total strangers will come up to you and ask you about your family, or they will know the name of your childhood pet, and this is disconcerting, but also fun. Fun, because they have read your work. And you are the dummy who decided to write a memoir, so deal with it.

STEVE ALMOND: Hey, your book is in the world. You did it. Try to take some pleasure in that achievement before proceeding to the compensatory shame and self-loathing.

HOW DOES WRITING ABOUT YOUR LIFE CHANGE YOUR LIFE?

FRANK MCCOURT: First of all, you get published. That's wonderful, to see your book in print. Then you're on television and on radio. People look at you in a different way: you're the guy who wrote the book, and for the first time in your life you have a bit of money, and some freedom, but with all of that, you want to go back and write.

ISHMAEL BEAH: In my case, the people who have read about my experience feel as if they know me very well and they are fresh in an experience that is in the past for me, that I have learned to live with.

SEAN WILSEY: I think you start to see how you could do things in real time that might later end up as a narrative you can write about, and that's weird. It's the inverse of what James Frey did. The honest man's version is to do stuff deliberately with the idea that you might write about it. And I think that's what certain memoirists/essayists (I'm thinking of David Sedaris, who's discussed this, and been very funny about it, and, in a serpent-eating-its-own-tail sort of way, made an entertaining, memoiristic narrative out of it) end up doing—creating real incidents as fodder for writing.

JONATHAN AMES: The course of my life has been completely affected by the fact that I'm a writer—the people who come into my life, the places I go; almost all of it is a result of this "career" as a writer, and my career, as a writer, has been partially built on writing about my life.

LAURA FRASER: It made me more well-known. Strange men wanted to go on dates with me so they could have their own affair. I think after the memoir I started viewing my life more as a story than I had before.

DAVID RAKOFF: I stay pretty vigilant about keeping the two separate. I'm already too self-conscious, I really don't want to further Heisenberg my complex human experiences by treating them as material. I find this distinction between the two really tremendously important.

AZADEH MOAVENI: It was like one enormous bout of venting that freed me permanently of a handful of preoccupations—identity, living between two worlds, biculturalism, etc. I'm grateful for this, but sometimes it's difficult because readers who are very much still in the throes of those issues really want to connect and talk about them, or hear me talk about them, and intellectually and emotionally I'm entirely elsewhere.

STEVE ALMOND: Hopefully, it makes you more forgiving, both of other people and yourself. We all do dumb and hurtful things, not because we're evil, but because our love somehow gets distorted. When you write a certain kind of nonfiction, you're trying to discover and trace those points where your love got whacked.

A.J. JACOBS: I once did a panel with a former Saturday Night Live writer named Alan Zweibel. I like what he said about this. He said that writers (or comics, I can't remember) go through life with two heads. One head is living the life, and the other head is hanging out on the shoulder observing it.

FIROOZEH DUMAS: I'm a much more relaxed, forgiving and grateful person. Writing gave me a lot of perspective. It made me more forgiving because, in writing about my family, I realized how often people do try to do the right thing, but fall short of my expectations. I am also somebody who has always needed a creative outlet. Lord knows I tried many things, but nothing fulfills me like writing. On days when I get to write, I'm calmer and more patient.

TAMIM ANSARY: It's a constant process. Every story starts to become false the moment it's frozen in time. Part of what I'm always doing is trying to escape from the story I shaped. I'm trying to get out of my own official story of myself. And when you write a memoir, that becomes even more the case. You petrify the self, but the self is not a petrified thing, so there's a constant tension there.

WHAT'S THE MOST IMPORTANT THING YOU'VE LEARNED FROM WRITING AND PUBLISHING YOUR MEMOIR?

BETH LISICK: It is an amazing feeling to get a note from a complete stranger who enjoyed reading what you wrote. Someone out there you have never met, someone with a complete life of their own, took the time to write and say thanks.

DAN KENNEDY: That I'm really alive and the meter is really running. The days are actually happening—they're real, they're going by, and one day I'll get to a very real and final version of the phrase "The End." I honestly sometimes am not sure it's the healthiest thing to be doing—the life examined is one thing, but I'm not entirely sure one doesn't pay a price for sitting there for two years mining their existence.

JONATHAN AMES: I'm pretty confused most of the time, whether or not I sound authoritative for the purposes of answering these questions. But that's what fuels my writing—my confusion. The epigraph for *Wake Up, Sir!* was a quotation from the narrator: "Live and don't learn—that's my motto."

MATTHUE ROTH: The adage about being a writer is that it's so hard, the only people who write are the ones who can't do anything else. I think memoirists are a subcategory of that idea: memoirists are the people who try to lie, who try to duck responsibility and make up stories about someone else. And they can't do anything about it. They have to tell the truth.

LAURA FRASER: Before I wrote the memoir, I always wrote hard journalism, serious reported articles. I didn't know I had a more sensuous storytelling voice. It was only because I allowed myself to write without expectations of getting published that I was able to find that voice.

Before then, I think I was always trying too hard. The voice in *An Italian Affair* came very naturally, because it was very personal. I guess I would say that sometimes you have to get out of the way of your own writing.

STEVE ALMOND: The path to truth—even beauty—leads through shame. Run toward it, and make sure your pen keeps moving.

PAUL COLLINS: A memoir is not a life. People will feel as if they know you: they don't. What they will know, hopefully, is a greater empathy for others, and that is a profound and worthy thing. But do not write in hopes of being personally understood. No one will know you through your memoir. They can only get to know you through … you. And that's why a few months after your book is out, your life will be almost exactly as it was before. Depending on your life, you may consider this a blessing or a disappointment. That's the strangest thing about writing books: it changes other people's lives, but not your own.

JANICE ERLBAUM: I've learned that publishing a book is only the beginning of a writing career, not the happy ending I thought it would be. I kind of thought that I'd publish a book, and then I'd be somehow "set for life"—emotionally, if not financially. But you've got to keep writing, and keep earning a living by other means, and keep deriving satisfaction from your work; there's no resting on your laurels.

CAROLINE KRAUS: I think it's helped me tremendously to finish a book, to hit all of the walls and frustrations and make it through to the other side. So much of writing is persistence—persistence, endurance, and routine. And it's so important to stay at it every day and long enough, because eventually the process delivers, and the long-await-ed connections emerge. Suddenly, or slowly, a cohesive story appears, and you can't figure out how it got there. I learned that's magic worth waiting for.

FIROOZEH DUMAS: Writing the memoir was one of the best things I ever did for myself and for my family. Getting published was icing on the cake but it was the actual act of writing that brought me the satisfaction. People think that getting published, like losing weight, will bring magic into one's life. Yes, getting published is exciting but it also exposes you to the business end of the book world, which can be ugly and frustrating.

A.J. JACOBS: I don't know. I think what I say is going to sound all cheesy, like something you'd say while sitting cross-legged in a circle at an est [Erhard Seminars Training] seminar. But I think the memoir has made me more connected to my emotions. The very act of writing about them forces me to pinpoint them and deal with them.

TANYA SHAFFER: The most important thing was proving to myself that I could finish such a sustained project. A book is mammoth. It was nine years from the time I returned from Africa and the time my book was published. Along the way there were many periods when I was focused on other projects and neglected it for months and even years. Many times I doubted the book would ever be done. Self-discipline has always been a struggle for me; seeing this project through to completion gave me an underlying faith in myself that carries over to other projects. And, ironically, having that faith makes it easier to get myself to the table. In spite of all the obstacles, the largest of which was probably my own difficulty in sticking to the task, I did it.

FROM THE MIND, TO THE INTERNET, TO THE BOOK, TO YOU

How people become bloggers and how blogs become books

There's one other memoir format you might want to consider, especially if you'd like more immediate gratification and greater autonomy: the blog. Blogs offer a lot of advantages—they're cheap, easy, and immediate, and you alone are in charge. There's no need to worry about chapters, narrative arcs, agents or editors. Blogs are incredibly interactive, letting you hear from your readers seconds after you post. And they're fluid; you can constantly revise and republish, documenting your life as you live it.

Blogs can also lead to more traditional publication. The daily discipline of blog-writing teaches you how to meet a deadline, and constant feedback lets you edit as you go. A blog may also bring you to the attention of agents and publishers. Several memoirs published in the past few years began, in fact, as blogs.

Of course, a blog can also be what prevents *you from getting your book written. Daily blog posts can be a tremendous distraction, and may drain resources you would otherwise save for the printed page.*

Still, for many, it works; here, a few blogger-cum-authors share what they've learned.

MEET OUR BLOG PANELISTS

KARYN BOSNAK

Karyn Bosnak is the author of *Save Karyn: One Shopaholic's Journey to Debt and Back*, based on her widely-read blog of the same name. She currently authors the blog Pretty in the City (*prettyinthecity.blogspot.com*), and is also the author of a novel, *Twenty Times a Lady*.

STEPHANIE KLEIN

Stephanie Klein is the author of *Straight Up and Dirty*, a memoir of recovering from a divorce, and is currently working on her second memoir, *MOOSE*, based on her experiences at fat camp. She is also known for her widely-read blog, "Greek Tragedy" (*stephanieklein.blogs.com*).

WENDY McCLURE

Wendy McClure is the author of the dieting memoir *I'm Not the New Me* and *The Amazing Mackerel Pudding Plan*. Her very popular blogs include Pound (*poundy.com*) and Candyboots (*candyboots.com*).

MELISSA PLAUT

Melissa Plaut is the author of *Hack: How I Stopped Worrying About What to Do with My Life and Started Driving a Yellow Cab*, based on her popular blog, New York Hack (*newyorkhack.blogspot.com*).

HOW A BLOG BECOMES A BOOK

WENDY McCLURE: There's this idea that the blog-to-book path is sort of a Cinderella story—that you're just blithely blogging along and one day you get this magical email with a book deal offer. That wasn't the case with me. First there was an early, failed attempt: a friend had gotten me in touch with an editor who liked my work, but at the time, in early 2001, publishers were much more cautious about doing books based on online material—could they really sell stuff that had been on the Internet for free? That initial wariness forced me to consider ways in which I could expand my blog into a book without relying on the online material. So I started writing a lot of stuff that I chose *not* to put online—bits of backstory and deeper narrative, things that I didn't feel like "just throwing out there" on the Internet. I did this for more than two years. I occasionally got emails from interested agents or editors, but nothing really happened until I knew what kind of book *I* wanted to write, and I put together a rough proposal and found an agent on my own.

MELISSA PLAUT: Well, the blog started just as some photos for my friends. I wanted to take pictures of the things I saw while working my shifts driving a cab. In the "old days" this might have taken the form of a 'zine or something, but the whole blog thing was easier—and cheaper. When I sent the link to my friends, they wrote back asking for "more words." Slowly, I starting writing more and more about what happened during each shift when I got home from work at around five in the morning. I was too tired to be self-conscious about it, and it didn't matter anyway because it was just supposed to be these people who already knew and loved me reading it. I was inspired and excited by my experiences driving the cab and I wanted to write about it for my friends and family.

Within six months of starting it, the blog got popular. It all started when one of my friends suggested I email *Gothamist.com* (a website about New York City). To my surprise, they actually linked to it. The next thing I knew, *Gawker.com* was linking to it and I was being interviewed by the Associated Press. When the AP story came out, I saw that 30,000 people a day were hitting the site. It was a little intimidating, to say the least! I got a few thousand emails, among which were a few inquiries from literary agents and book editors. I asked myself if I could write a book, and if I even wanted to. I realized that I really did want to, that I had a longer story to tell that sort of encompassed all these smaller tidbits that happened in the cab. There were a lot of things I wanted to write about that I didn't feel comfortable sharing on a blog. I realized that, oddly enough, I would have more freedom writing a book than I did with a blog, mainly because it was much more private and much less immediate. I could write about the somewhat illegal things I did and I could honestly reveal things about myself and not worry about getting bombarded the very next day with angry or mean comments from people on the Internet.

I signed on with an agent and wrote a proposal. We sent it around to editors and the book got sold on the first day! The whole thing was, quite possibly, the luckiest progression of events to ever happen to a person. Who knew that when I started driving a taxi—which in New York is seen as the lowest form of employment—it would ultimately lead to a book deal with a major publisher! It was pretty awesome.

STEPHANIE KLEIN: In January of 2004, I was working full-time in advertising, and by night (and between business meetings) I was posting my angst online, frustrated that I didn't know how to make myself happy. As a New Year's resolution, I promised to write every day. Having a blog enabled me to create an online scrapbook of my life, complete with drawings, photos, and my daily musings. About five months later, the *Independent*, a newspaper in London, contacted me saying, "We're pissing ourselves over here, ya, and we want to publish your blog. We'll pay you, ya?" Uh, ya! So after being featured in their papers, I was offered a book deal from a U.K. publishing house. I declined the offer, found a U.S. literary agent, then worked on a book proposal for my first memoir, *Straight Up and Dirty*, inspired by the content on my blog. Since there was such an overwhelming response to the "dating after divorce" material I'd been writing on the blog, I decided to use some of it in the book, but mostly the blog simply served as a starting point. My agents sent out my book proposal on a Wednesday, and by Friday, I had eight meetings scheduled with different U.S. publishing houses. By Sunday afternoon, I had been offered a two-book deal with HarperCollins. I'm now working with NBC Universal, writing the pilot for the series based on *Straight Up and Dirty*, and gearing up for *MOOSE*, my fat-camp memoir.

KARYN BOSNAK: My website began in 2002, before the big "blog boom" took off. At that time, there was no Gawker, no Huffington Post, no Perez Hilton, etc. In fact, I remember being interviewed by someone who asked me what I got out of blogging and I replied, "What's blogging?" *SaveKaryn.com* was in fact a blog, but I never referred to it as that. It was just a website on which I kept a diary about the financial mess I had gotten myself into and the progress I was making getting out of it.

As far as blog-to-book deals, I've never done the research, but I think I might be one of the first. It all came about like this: I received an e-mail from someone at Penguin Putnam in August 2002 asking me if I had given any thought to writing a book about my experiences because they liked my website and writing style. I had, in fact, thought about it, so I asked a friend who happened to work at an agency how I should proceed. She set up a meeting for me with the literary agent there, who ended up loving my story and was on the same page with me with regards to the kind of book I wanted to write, that is, a memoir that read like fiction. It took me about a week to write my proposal.

When I was finished, my agent sent it out to a few editors at different publishing houses. At the time, *SaveKaryn.com* was getting a lot of press, so the editors wanted to meet me in person, which was kind of cool because I had never been to a publishing house before. I clicked with everyone at HarperCollins instantly, particularly the person who ended up being my editor. After all the meetings, they were the first ones to make an offer and we took it. It was a good fit.

ADVICE FOR THE ASPIRING
BLOGGER–MEMOIRIST

STEPHANIE KLEIN: Be honest. Write as if no one else will read your words. The moment you begin to censor yourself, you stray from the truth. And the truth is rarely boring.

Write often. Change names just before you publish your entry. Make sure you have thick skin and expect that the more well-known you become, the more loved, and the more Hated you'll become. Yes, capital H. If it's your intention to be published (other than online) spend your time working on a kick-ass book proposal.

MELISSA PLAUT: I would say to just be brave and honest and try as hard as you can to ignore all the negative people on the Internet, because there are, unfortunately, a *lot* of them!

WENDY MCCLURE: Publishers love to say that a blog is a platform, but I think it's better to think of a blog as a process. It's where you figure out what your story is, your voice, your rhythm. Those are more important than developing a big following or having a brilliant persona. And if you want to write a book, know that you can't write it in that little "post to your blog" box in your web browser. A lot of great things happen there, but there's no way you're going to be able to push a whole book out of that little box. That thing is too damn small.

KARYN BOSNAK: Don't use all your material on your blog! It's a little like not giving it up on the first date—you know what I mean? You have to hold some things back so people come back for more. Remember, publishing is a business. No one is going to publish a book that's already on the Internet because no one's going to want to buy a book that's already on the Internet.

Find a distinctive niche—but make sure it's authentically you—and stick with it. By "authentically you," I mean, don't try to be something you're not simply to get traffic. People will read through your bullshit, tune out and never come back. Be unique, but be real.

ON OPENNESS AND INTERACTION

WENDY MCCLURE: I don't think blog writing requires any more openness than other memoir forms; I think it just feels that way because the readers are so much closer online. When you write for such an immediate audience, you tend to get back the same energy you put out there—if you *think* the thing you're sharing (or not sharing) is a Very Big Deal, readers are likely to think so, too. I've found people will respect personal boundaries as long as the boundaries are consistent, and they don't wonder about what I'm not telling them. Like that freaky thing that happened to me as a kid: I never talk about *that*.

MELISSA PLAUT: I was a little nervous and intimidated when people I didn't know started reading my blog. Before that it had just been this thing I wrote for me and my friends with the idea that no one was going to judge me too severely or anything.

When strangers started looking at the blog, I convinced myself to pretend that it was still just my friends reading it. The only time it became an issue for me was when people would write comments or emails that were mean or insulting. As much as I didn't want to let it bother me, it did. Some were so malicious, they made me consider shutting down the blog completely. It took a while, but I eventually learned to deal with it better and just focus on the positive feedback I was getting.

Another thing that helped was that I never got *too* personal on the blog. I didn't start it to write about my love life or my dysfunctional family or anything. I stayed on topic and wrote about the cool, weird, sometimes upsetting stuff that happened to me in my cab. Of course, if that involved some other part of my personal life, then I wrote about that too.

STEPHANIE KLEIN: I don't believe the writing itself of a blogger-memoirist is any more open than a traditional memoirist. Though, I do suppose we're more open in that we welcome a dialogue and allow readers to voice their thoughts, questions, irritations. We make ourselves available, which makes one think twice before publishing something online. "No way am I posting this today," I might say if my ego isn't ready to be berated by passionate readers. Or, I'll just disable comments.

In most other channels, readers don't often have such an immediately gratifying experience, to simply be able to tell the author exactly how what they read made them feel.

KARYN BOSNAK: I think books are more intimate than blogs; they have the ability to affect the reader on a deeper level and suck them in more. Because of this, I'd tease the more personal stuff on the blog but not write it. Let readers know that there might be more to a particular story, but don't necessarily tell them what it is. And don't give in to the pressure to tell them, either! By this I mean: blog readers can be rather needy. I mean this in the kindest way because bloggers would be nowhere without their readers. But I'm a blog reader myself, so I know: blog readers can be rather needy.

My point in all this is this: Don't let pressure from readers convince you to tell a whole story if you don't want to tell it or are not ready to tell it. Give what you are comfortable giving ... and save the good stuff for the book!

ON SWITCHING FROM BLOG FORMAT TO BOOK FORMAT

WENDY McCLURE: There's a huge shift in perspective. When you're writing for a book you're no longer in the day-to-day or week-to-week grind of blog writing, and that can be very freeing. But sometimes material that worked perfectly well in a blog feels considerably less significant within the more expansive context of a book, and suddenly you'll find yourself wondering, "Is this important enough?" At first it's all very *Alice In Wonderland*, where the doors keep changing size, but you eventually adjust.

STEPHANIE KLEIN: They are two completely different animals. Oftentimes, I believe agents and publishers are wary of taking a chance with a blogger, however popular, because writing a book uses a different set of skills. Blog writing needs to satisfy quickly. The online world is impatient. Readers don't want to scroll through pages, so a blogger learns to be concise, to get to the point, even if rushed. Perhaps a single post has a theme, its own beginning, middle, and end. But many bloggers aren't sure where to begin if asked to compose a book, even if it's based on the same material as their blog. Books need an arc, a beginning, middle, and end. I'd say the biggest difference between blog writing and book writing is vision and the ability to wrap yourself around structure. You cannot simply have the sauce; you have to know how to spread it.

MELISSA PLAUT: I was writing a lot of new stuff for the book that never got covered in the blog, so that created the biggest challenge right there. There were a handful of stories that I wrote for the blog that I really wanted in the book and I had to figure out how make them fit into the larger narrative somehow. I also had to drop the punchline-y endings that worked so well on the blog. In the book, they were just like, "ba-dum-bum," and interfered with the transitions, so I ended up just starting over and totally rewriting a lot of them.

KARYN BOSNAK: Your book can't be a replica of your blog—and not just because people have already read your blog on the Internet. Books read much differently from blogs. Blog posts can be disjointed. One doesn't need to have anything to do with the next. In a book, however, you need a narrative that connects one paragraph or chapter to the next. There needs to be a "through-story" that strings and holds everything together, and this through-story needs to have a beginning, a middle, and an end. It can be challenging to find this, but it's absolutely necessary.

Also, something should be said about unpublished posts. I've never asked other bloggers about this, but am I only one who has a gazillion half-written, unpublished posts saved to my blog? I seriously have over 200 of them. Most are unpublished because I couldn't completely wrap my head around a thought, or maybe I felt like I was giving too much of myself. But they're like a diary. And they're like gold.

HOW DOES THE DISCIPLINE
OF REGULAR BLOG POSTING
CHANGE YOUR WRITING?

WENDY MCCLURE: I wouldn't call my blog posting disciplined by any stretch of the imagination, but I think it has helped. For several years—just before I started writing online—the only personal writing I did were these scribbly, incoherent stream-of-consciousness journal entries. They were unfocused and twitchy, and while they weren't worthless they didn't really say much, making me feel I'd lost the ability to communicate, even to myself. Somehow the idea of an audience helped ground me.

STEPHANIE KLEIN: So often I'll read something by another author, journalist, writer, and I'll think, "See, I should be writing like that. That is good stuff." What blogging has enabled me to see is people actually like my voice, as it is. I needn't try to change it, to be more serious or contemplative. Blogging has freed me up and has lifted some of my self-imposed pressure. It has also enabled me to distinguish my good writing from my crap writing, where I take the easy way out. I begin to see patterns and am able to realize when I could be pushing myself further.

MELISSA PLAUT: It helped my writing tremendously, first because I would write every time I drove the cab, and that gave me discipline to begin with. There was also the satisfaction of seeing it online immediately and knowing somebody somewhere was reading it—even if it was just my mom or dad (although they were eventually forbidden to read it)—and that inspired me to write even more. Most importantly, it put me in touch with my "writing voice" or whatever you want to call it. From writing so regularly and without getting too neurotic about it, I developed a stronger sense of my own style and tone and felt more comfortable writing for other people and revealing more about myself.

The only drawbacks were those punchy endings I fell so in love with. I had to get rid of those and figure out a better way to create transitions without relying on the crutch of a joke to finish off each story.

KARYN BOSNAK: I was never a "writer" before my first website. When I started writing on *SaveKaryn.com*, I didn't think anyone was reading. Because of this, I didn't really pay much attention to the little things ... like, um, *grammar*. (Ha ha.) I wrote (and still write) like I talk, like I'm having a conversation with someone. This is both good and bad. Writing without thinking that anyone is reading has helped me to cultivate my own "voice," but that voice can sometimes come across as being ... uneducated. When no one was reading *SaveKaryn.com*, I never changed these little errors. In fact, I kind of liked them because they were uniquely my own. (Ha ha.) But as more people started reading my blog (and eventually books), more people started commenting about and pointing out my mistakes. With all these comments floating around in the back of my mind, I started going back and changing things more and more.

My writing has evolved because of this, mostly in a good way—the things I write make more sense now and are easier to understand—but all this going back and changing things has muddled up my mind a bit. Writing and editing are two different processes. I write with the creative side of the brain (right side) and edit with the logical side (left side). Sometimes when I'm writing and I'm in total right-brain mode, the left side will catch something and kill my train of thought. I hate this. More than anything. But whatever.

In short, regular blog posting has made me a better writer. I pay more attention to the little things, like, um, yes, *grammar* ... but sometimes this can be irritating. Another thing about blog posting: It has made me more cautious, more aware of the reader. Again, I think this is both good and bad. I know who my audience is now, and that's a good thing. But if I let this audience start to dictate what I'm writing (even subconsciously), that would be a tragedy.

CONCLUSION

Inward and Onward

Well, that's it. The best advice we have to offer. If the accumulated wisdom of the world's best memoirists can't get you motivated and ready to write your own, what will?

Then again, exercises—hands-on and specific—can be a boon and a boost. Jennifer Traig has come up with exercises corresponding to every one of the chapters in this book, and they're all available online. They cover everything from pushing through a period of unspiration to finding your ideal first reader. They're encouraging and demystifying and are available here:

http://us.macmillan.com/theautobiographershandbook

We hope the exercises, in concert with the voices of our brain trust, will give you the courage and expertise to write your story. The world awaits it, and we encourage it. We thank you for listening to us as we wait to listen to you.

APPENDIX

A PERSONAL HISTORY
OF THE MEMOIR

Highlights in the annals of autobiography

Self-reflective and confessional, the memoir seems the most modern of forms, but it's actually quite ancient, as old as memory itself. There are Biblical memoirs, Medieval autobiographies, and Elizabethan tell-alls. A brief history of the evolution of the genre:

The Book of Ecclesiastes

(ca. 250 B.C.E.)

The most autobiographical book of the Bible, the Book of Ecclesiastes is an early masterpiece of self-reflective literature. Its authorship is debated, and is sometimes assigned to King Solomon. Reads like *Harlot's Ghost*-era Norman Mailer.

Libanius's *Orations*

(ca. 200 C.E.)

This is a perfect example of the memoir as the ancient Greeks and Romans understood it: a memo, or note to self, an unfinished work the author wrote primarily to help remember things that he wanted to write about later.

The Confessions of Saint Augustine
(397–98 C.E.)

Generally considered the first autobiography, this collection of thirteen books covers the author's dissolute youth and conversion to Christianity, and contains the line from which Oscar Wilde borrowed endlessly and extrapolated upon: "Grant me chastity and continence, but not yet."

Sei Shonagon's *Pillow Book*
(ca. 900 C.E.)

Written at the turn of the tenth century, this free-form collection of reminiscences chronicles the author's life as a lady-in-waiting. Fewer dirty parts than the title might suggest.

The Life of Saint Theresa of Avila by Herself
(ca. 1567)

The invention of the printing press meant more memoirs, and customs of the day meant that the majority were religious in tone. More charming and less pedantic than its peers, this one is the best-known and best-liked, and was, with Saint Augustine's *Confessions*, considered one of the two most important autobiographies until the eighteenth century.

The Diary of Samuel Pepys
(1660–69)

Not a memoir per se, this is nonetheless an outstanding personal history of the English Restoration period. Although Pepys didn't write it for publication—it was written for his own personal use, in a shorthand called tachygraphy—he clearly wrote it for posterity, a goal achieved with the diary's transcription and publication in 1825. Not to be missed: the author's account of having kidney stones removed without benefit of anesthesia.

The Confessions of Jean-Jacques Rousseau

(1782)

The first true modern memoir, this work focuses not on the author's spirituality but on his life in the world. It also, rather modernly, includes plenty of humiliating and embarrassing anecdotes. A truly innovative work, it would prove influential on writers like Tolstoy and Goethe as well as *Seventeen* magazine's *Trauma-Rama: Life's Most Embarrassing Moments ... and How to Deal.*

Giacomo Casanova's *Histoire de ma vie*

(1797)

In the eighteenth century memoir-writing took a turn for the spicy, as libertines and ladies of the night churned out a number of scandalous memoirs. Unsurprisingly, these proved very popular. Casanova's contribution may be the best-known example, recounting the author's dalliances with 122 women.

Narrative of the Life of Frederick Douglass, an American Slave, Written by Himself

(1845)

A number of slave memoirs were written in the mid–nineteenth century. This, the best-known, was hugely influential in advancing the abolitionist movement. Also of note: *Memoir* and *Poems of Phyllis Wheatley, a Native African and Slave* (1834). The first African-American woman author, Wheatley had to defend her talents in court against challengers who refused to believe a black woman could write so beautifully.

Henry David Thoreau's *Walden*

(1854)

Still hugely influential, this classic more or less invented the form of personal nonfiction all writers would emulate through today. Though it seems to take place over a single year, it actually took Thoreau eight years to write, and he lived with his mom. He also started an absolutely massive forest fire.

Walt Whitman's "Song of Myself"

(1855)

Memoir as poetry, it celebrates self-love—self as embodiment of life. Hugely popular in his time, Whitman rubbed some readers the wrong way, particularly Mark Twain, who objected to Whitman's use of the royal "we." Twain surmised that the "we" must refer to Whitman and his tapeworm.

Mark Twain's *The Innocents Abroad*

(1869)

Twain was a busy man. Considered the father of the Great American Novel, he also originated Self-Deprecating American Personal Humor. In *Innocents* he originates two major forms: the humorous memoir and the travel memoir, a formula he would repeat in *Roughing It* and *A Tramp Abroad*, and which would be repeated by others, again and again, for the next hundred-odd years.

Gertrude Stein's *The Autobiography of Alice B. Toklas*

(1933)

Not, in fact, of Alice at all, these are Stein's memoirs as recounted through Toklas's viewpoint. The most codependent memoir ever written, it is also the most self-congratulatory, containing numerous references to Stein's own genius. In spite of this, it's entirely engaging and likeable, like Stein herself.

George Orwell's *Down and Out in Paris and London*

(1933)

Aspiring memoirists short on funds and material take note: when Orwell couldn't support himself freelancing, he reluctantly took a series of menial jobs, which ended up providing the stories for this book. Problem solved. The book is also noteworthy for incorporating memoir and political philosophy.

Anne Frank's *The Diary of a Young Girl*
(1947)

Like Pepys's diary, it was not written for publication, but in moving fashion does what all good memoirs do: records a personal life in a larger public moment.

Mary McCarthy's *Memoirs of a Catholic Girlhood*
(1957)

Entirely innovative, this is memoir with all its seams showing: at the end of each chapter, McCarthy deconstructs the narrative, presenting the actual facts and explaining why she deviated from them. Required reading for aspiring memoirists.

Alex Haley's *The Autobiography of Malcolm X*
(1965)

Based on interviews conducted shortly before Malcolm X's death, the book describes Malcolm X's political and philosophical development and is considered one of the most important nonfiction books of the twentieth century.

Maxine Hong Kingston's
The Woman Warrior: Memoir of a Girlhood Among Ghosts
(1975)

With this seminal work, Hong Kingston originated Asian-American literature. She also invented a poetic memoir style that combines auto-biography, magical realism, and myth.

Richard Rodriguez's
Hunger of Memory: The Education of Richard Rodriguez
(1982)

Innovative for its form (essays) and subject (assimilation, affirmative action, and bilingual education). Gorgeously written and politically charged, it remains hugely relevant and important.

Shirley Maclaine's *Out on a Limb*
(1983)

In the '70s and early '80s—maybe it was all the drugs—memoirs took a turn for the spiritual. This one, along with Richard Bach's *Illusions: Adventures of a Reluctant Messiah*, are two of the best-known and best-selling. At least one of them is on your basement bookshelf right now.

Julia Phillips's *You'll Never Eat Lunch in This Town Again*
(1991)

The '80s and '90s saw some wonderful genre-defining literary memoirs— like Russell Baker's *Growing Up*; Annie Dillard's *An American Childhood*; Susanna Kaysen's *Girl, Interrupted*; Lucy Grealy's *Autobiography of a Face*; and Mary Karr's *Liars' Club*—but the era is probably better known for dishy celebrity tell-alls like this one.

Elizabeth Wurtzel's *Prozac Nation*
(1994)

A generation-defining work, *Prozac Nation* paved the way for the confessional, even solipsistic memoir that became popular for the next ten years and counting.

Frank McCourt's *Angela's Ashes*
(1996)

Everyone read this book. Which may have led, in part, to...

The Bumper Crop of Millennial Memoirs
(2000–PRESENT)

The turn of the millennium ended up being the Age of Memoir. Maybe it had something to do with the demand for authenticity and authority in an age of mechanical reproduction and binary identities. Maybe it's about the rise of the individual, or a communal need for confession. Whatever the reason, it brings us to you, and now, and the telling of your story.

HISTORY'S STRANGEST
ACTUAL MEMOIRS

Compiled by Paul Collins

George Psalmanazar's *Memoirs of ****, Commonly Known by the*
Name of George Psalmanazar; a Reputed Native of Formosa
(1764)

Psalmanazar's confession of how he sponged off London's elite in 1704 by passing himself of as a native of the exotic, mysterious and then little-known island of Taiwan. How little-known was it? Well, the fact that George was blond didn't tip anyone off.

Timothy Dexter's *A Pickle for The Knowing Ones*
(1798)

An eccentric speculator who erected wooden statues of himself on the front lawn and kept his very own "poet laureate" in tow to write his praises, Dexter faked his own death just to hear the nice eulogies. He then got mad because his wife didn't seem too sad about the loss.

The Memoir of Zerah Colburn
(1833)

Zerah was a five-year-old mathematical prodigy with the misfortune to have the original stage dad. Endless European stump-the-boy-genius tours followed. Strangest moment: an audience member asking Zerah for the exact date of when the world will end.

Edward Tippett's *Experiences and Trials*
(1833)

The memoirs of a perpetually broke perpetual-motion enthusiast. He was fond of pestering President Andrew Jackson by mail with fully-transcribed accounts of dreams he'd had the night before.

James Holbrook's *Ten Years Among the Mail Bags: or, Notes from the Diary of a Special Agent of the Post-Office Department*
(1855)

Holbrook tried to trap a mail-theft suspect by taking him out bowling, hoping that a friendly bet would produce a stolen marked bill from the suspect's wallet. Unfortunately, the suspect proved to be an excellent bowler.

Francis Tumblety's *A Few Passages in the Life of Dr. Francis Tumblety, The Indian Herb Doctor*
(1866)

An indignant rant by a quack mistakenly jailed on suspicion of conspiring in Abraham Lincoln's assassination. Tumblety later moved to London and promptly became a suspect in the Jack the Ripper murders.

Ike Matthews's *Full Revelations of a Professional Rat Catcher*
(1898)

Ike's favorite trick of the trade: on a moonlit night, run a trail of oatmeal out of an infested barn. Then, get behind a haystack and wait with a rifle.

Al Jennings's *Through the Shadows with O.Henry*
(1921)

When the great short story writer was on the lam for embezzlement, Jennings was his fellow fugitive. Picture *O Brother, Where Art Thou?*, but with handlebar moustaches.

Charles Kellogg's *The Nature Singer*

(1929)

Kellogg invented the RV in 1914 by hollowing out a giant redwood into a bed, bath, and kitchen, and then mounting this Flintstonian contraption on a truck chassis. He also claimed the ability of putting out fires by singing—certainly a useful talent in a wooden kitchen.

David Goulet's *Looney Tombs:*
Confessions of a Small Town Funeral Director's Son

(2000)

Here's sage advice: don't defrost dead vagrants in the family bathtub.

ACTUAL MEMOIR TITLES CONSIDERED AND REJECTED

by this book's contributors

Steve Almond's *Candyfreak: A Journey through the Chocolate Underbelly of America*
- *Chocolate Psychotic: Why I Have No Teeth in My Head*

Jonathan Ames's *My Less Than Secret Life*
- *The Herring Wonder*

A.J. Jacobs's *The Know-It-All: One Man's Humble Quest to Become the Smartest Person in the World*
- *From Aardvark to Zygote: One Man's Adventure through the Alphabet*
- *Thomas Jefferson Has Clean Feet (and other things I learned while reading the encyclopedia)*
- *René Descartes Had a Fetish for Cross-Eyed Women (and other things I learned in the Britannica)*

Dan Kennedy's *Loser Goes First*
- *Evidently I Know Everything*
- *Green*

David Rakoff's *Fraud*
- *The Jig Is Up*
- *Smarty Pants*
- *Shut Up, You Stupid Jew Fag!*
- *It Tastes Like Chicken*

Jennifer Traig's *Devil in the Details: Scenes from an Obsessive Girlhood*
- *Wait, Wait—There are a Whole Lot More Things Wrong with Me*

RECOMMENDED READING

The best way to learn how to write a great memoir is to read one. Fortunately, there are hundreds of wonderful memoirs to choose from. Here are just a few. They're organized by category, and it's maybe helpful to read the memoirs that sound most like your own.

This is by no means a definitive list of all great memoirs. It does not include, for instance, yours. But we hope someday it will.

CANONICAL MEMOIRS

I Know Why the Caged Bird Sings, Maya Angelou
Growing Up, Russell Baker
An American Childhood, Annie Dillard
The Woman Warrior, Maxine Hong Kingston
Memories of a Catholic Girlhood, Mary McCarthy
Angela's Ashes, Frank McCourt
Hunger of Memory, Richard Rodriguez
This Boy's Life, Tobias Wolff

MEMOIRS ABOUT UNUSUAL LIVES

Boy, Roald Dahl
Borrowed Finery, Paula Fox
I Am Not Myself These Days, Josh Kilmer-Purcell
The Color of Water, James McBride

Palimpsest, Gore Vidal
The Glass Castle, Jeannette Walls
Oh, the Glory of It All, Sean Wilsey
Duke of Deception, Geoffrey Wolff

MEMOIRS OF NORMAL LIVES

A Girl Named Zippy, Haven Kimmel
The Discomfort Zone, Jonathan Franzen
Everybody Into the Pool, Beth Lisick
Encyclopedia of an Ordinary Life, Amy Krouse Rosenthal

FUNNY MEMOIRS

I'm a Stranger Here Myself, Bill Bryson
Running with Scissors, Augusten Burroughs
Funny in Farsi, Firoozeh Dumas
Loser Goes First, Dan Kennedy
Confessions of a Failed Southern Lady, Florence King
Naked, David Sedaris

MEMOIRS THAT DEFTLY TACKLE HARD TOPICS

Another Bullshit Night in Suck City, Nick Flynn
8, Amy Fusselman
The Kiss, Kathryn Harrison
The Man Who Outgrew His Prison Cell, Joe Loya
Lucky, Alice Sebold
Bastard Out of Carolina, Dorothy Allison

MEMOIRS ABOUT LOSS

Here if You Need Me, Kate Braestrup
The Year of Magical Thinking, Joan Didion
The Lost Night, Rachel Howard

MEMOIRS ABOUT LOVE

The Turkish Lover, Esmeralda Santiago
By Grand Central Station I Sat Down and Wept, Elizabeth Smart
First Comes Love, Marion Winik

MEMOIRS ABOUT UNDERTAKING
A CHALLENGE OR EXPERIMENT

The Know-It-All and *The Year of Living Biblically*, A.J. Jacobs
Positively Fifth Street and *Physical: An American Checkup*, James
    McManus
Julie and Julia, Julie Powell
Early Bird, Rodney Rothman
Opening Skinner's Box, Lauren Slater
Ambulance Girl, Jane Stern
Self Made Man, Norah Vincent

MEMOIRS ABOUT TRANSFORMATION

She's Not There, Jennifer Finney Boylan
Passing for Thin, Frances Kuffel

MEMOIRS ABOUT ADDICTION AND RECOVERY

Drinking: A Love Story, Carolyn Knapp
Permanent Midnight, Jerry Stahl
More, Now, Again, Elizabeth Wurtzel

FOOD MEMOIRS

Candyfreak, Steve Almond
Heat, Bill Buford
My Life in France, Julia Child
The Art of Eating, M.F.K. Fisher
My Kitchen Wars, Betty Fussell
Cooking for Mr. Latte, Amanda Hesser

Animal, Vegetable, Miracle, Barbara Kingsolver
Candy and Me, Hilary Liftin
Comfort Me with Apples, Tender at the Bone, and *Garlic and Sapphires*, Ruth Reichl
Toast, Nigel Slater

TRAVEL MEMOIRS

Neither Here nor There, In a Sunburned Country, and *A Walk in the Woods*, Bill Bryson
Looking Forward to It, Stephen Elliott
An Italian Affair, Laura Fraser
Eat, Pray, Love, Elizabeth Gilbert
Somebody's Heart is Burning, Tanya Shaffer
Travels with Charlie, John Steinbeck

MEMOIRS ABOUT PLACE

Where I Was From, Joan Didion
Sixpence House, Paul Collins

MEMOIRS ABOUT MOVING BETWEEN WORLDS

West of Kabul, East of New York, Tamim Ansary
'Tis, Frank McCourt
The Woman Warrior, Maxine Hong Kingston
Chasing Hepburn, Gus Lee
Lipstick Jihad, Azadeh Moaveni
When I was Puerto Rican, Esmeralda Santiago

MEMOIRS ABOUT FAMILY

Sweet and Low, Rich Cohen
Not Even Wrong, Paul Collins
Brother, I'm Dying, Edwidge Danticat
Operating Instructions, Anne Lamott

Ace of Spades, David Matthews
Running in the Family, Michael Ondaatje
The Kid, Dan Savage
West of Then, Tara Bray Smith
Brothers and Keepers, John Edgar Wideman

MEMOIRS ABOUT COMING OUT

How I Learned to Snap, Kirk Read
Chelsea Whistle, Michelle Tea

MEMOIRS ABOUT FAITH

The Spiral Staircase, Karen Armstrong
Foreskin's Lament, Shalom Auslander
This Dark World, Carolyn S. Briggs
Traveling Mercies, Anne Lamott
Vows, Peter Manseau
Yom Kippur a Go-Go, Matthue Roth
Jesus Land, Julia Scheeres

MEMOIRS ABOUT ADOLESCENCE

Lake Effect, Rich Cohen
Girlbomb: A Halfway Homeless Memoir, Janice Erlbaum
Almost a Woman, Esmeralda Santiago

MEMOIRS ABOUT FRIENDSHIP

Dear Exile, Hilary Liftin and Kate Montgomery
Truth and Beauty, Ann Patchett

MEMOIRS ABOUT WAR

Hello to All That, John Falk
Jarhead, Anthony Swofford
In Pharaoh's Army, Tobias Wolff

MEMOIRS ABOUT WORK

Blue Blood, Edward Conlon
But Enough About Me, Jancee Dunn
Teacher Man, Frank McCourt

MEMORIES ABOUT THE BODY AND ILLNESS

At the Will of the Body, Arthur Frank
Autobiography of a Face, Lucy Grealy
Sickened, Julie Gregory
Time on Fire, Evan Handler
All in My Head, Paula Kamen
Fat Girl, Judith Moore

PSYCHIATRIC MEMOIRS

Girl, Interrupted, Susanna Kaysen
Borderlines, Caroline Kraus
The Bell Jar, Sylvia Plath
The Noonday Demon, Andrew Solomon
Welcome to My Country and *Prozac Diary*, Lauren Slater
Darkness Visible, William Styron
Passing for Normal, Amy S. Wilensky

PERSONAL ESSAYS

(Not That You Asked), Steve Almond
What's Not to Love, My Less Than Secret Life, and *I Love You More Than
    You Know*, Jonathan Ames
My Misspent Youth, Meghan Daum
Slouching Towards Bethlehem and *The White Album*, Joan Didion
Ex Libris and *At Large and at Small*, Anne Fadiman
How to Be Alone, Jonathan Franzen
Portrait of My Body, Getting Personal, and *The Art of the Personal Essay*,
    Philip Lopate

Fraud and *Don't Get Too Comfortable*, David Rakoff
Me Talk Pretty One Day, David Sedaris
Take the Cannoli, *The Partly Cloudy Patriot*, and *Assassination Vacation*,
   Sarah Vowell
A Supposedly Fun Thing I'll Never Do Again, David Foster Wallace

BOOKS BY BLOGGERS

Save Karyn: One Shopaholic's Journey to Debt and Back, Karyn Bosnak
Straight Up and Dirty, Stephanie Klein
I'm Not the New Me, Wendy McClure
Hack, Melissa Plaut
Julie and Julia, Julie Powell

GRAPHIC MEMOIRS

Fun Home, Alison Bechdel
Monkey Food and *I Love Led Zeppelin*, Ellen Forney
The Diary of a Teenage Girl, Phoebe Gloeckner
Hoochie Mama, Erika Lopez
Persepolis, Marjane Satrapi
Maus, Art Spiegelman

AUTOBIOGRAPHICAL NOVELS

Happy Baby, Stephen Elliott
Valencia, Michelle Tea
China Boy and *Honor and Duty*, Gus Lee

BOOKS ON MEMOIR

Enough About You, David Shields
Inventing the Truth, William Zinsser, ed.

BOOKS ABOUT WRITING

The Artists' Way, Julia Cameron
Writing Down the Bones, Natalie Goldberg
Bird by Bird, Anne Lamott
This Year You Write Your Novel, Walter Mosley
On Writing Well, William Zinsser

ACKNOWLEDGEMENTS

Thank you, thank you

826 Valencia runs on the big-hearted benevolence of thousands of volunteers, contributors, and supporters. Here are just a few who were especially helpful with this project: Elissa Bassist; Brian McMullen; Sona Avakian; Amy Yelin; Robert Mickey; Trevor Koski; Christopher Benz; Darren Franich; M. Rebekah Otto; Chris Ying; Michelle Quint; Ted Weinstein; and the generous and talented authors who shared their invaluable ideas with us here.

ABOUT THE EDITOR

Jennifer Traig

Jennifer Traig is the author of two memoirs: *Well Enough Alone*, a personal history of hypochondria; and *Devil in the Details*, an account of her adolescence as an obsessive-compulsive religious fanatic. A longtime tutor at 826 Valencia, Jennifer has a Ph.D. in Literature and lives in Berkeley, California.

ABOUT 826 NATIONAL

Proceeds from this book benefit youth literacy

A large percentage of the cover price of this book goes to 826 National, a network of ten youth tutoring, writing, and publishing centers in seven cities around the country.

Since the birth of 826 National in 2002, our goal has been to assist students ages 6–18 with their writing skills while helping teachers get their classes passionate about writing. We do this with a vast army of volunteers who donate their time so we can give as much one-on-one attention as possible to the students whose writing needs it. Our mission is based on the understanding that great leaps in learning can happen with one-on-one attention, and that strong writing skills are fundamental to future success.

Through volunteer support, each of the seven 826 chapters — in San Francisco, New York, Los Angeles, Ann Arbor, Chicago, Seattle, and Boston — provides drop-in tutoring, class field trips, writing workshops, and in-schools programs, all free of charge, for students, classes, and schools. 826 centers are especially committed to supporting teachers, offering services and resources for English Language Learners, and publishing student work. Each of the 826 chapters works to produce professional-quality publications written entirely by young people, to forge relationships with teachers in order to create innovative workshops and lesson plans, to inspire students to write and appreciate the written word, and to rally thousands of enthusiastic volunteers to make it all happen.

By offering all of our programming for free, we aim to serve families who cannot afford to pay for the level of personalized instruction their children receive through 826 chapters.

The demand for 826 National's services is tremendous. Last year we worked with more than 4,000 volunteers and over 18,000 students nationally, hosted 368 field trips, completed 170 major in-schools projects, offered 266 evening and weekend workshops, welcomed over 130 students per day for after-school tutoring, and produced over 600 student publications. At many of our centers, our field trips are fully booked almost a year in advance, teacher requests for in-school tutor support continue to rise, and the majority of our evening and weekend workshops have waitlists.

826 National volunteers are local community residents, professional writers, teachers, artists, college students, parents, bankers, lawyers, and retirees from a wide range of professions. These passionate individuals can be found at all of our centers after school, sitting side-by-side with our students, providing one-on-one attention. They can be found running our field trips, or helping an entire classroom of local students learn how to write a story, or assisting student writers during one of our Young Authors' Book Programs.

All day and in a variety of ways, our volunteers are actively connecting with youth from the communities we serve.

To learn more or get involved, please visit:

826 National: www.826national.org
826 in San Francisco: www.826valencia.org
826 in New York: www.826nyc.org
826 in Los Angeles: www.826la.org
826 in Chicago: www.826chi.org
826 in Ann Arbor: www.826mi.org
826 in Seattle: www.826seattle.org
826 in Boston: www.826boston.org